# TAKING THE ORFF APPROACH TO HEART

ESSAYS & ARTICLES FROM A PIONEER OF ORFF IN AMERICA

SECOND EDITION

ISABEL MCNEILL CARLEY

Edited by

ANNE M CARLEY

BRASSTOWN PRESS

Brasstown Press
Charlottesville, VA
brasstownpress.com

Second edition, 2025
ISBN 978-1-931922-09-8
Printed in USA

# CONTENTS

# FOREWORD

Although I never met her, Isabel McNeill Carley has been an inspiration to my teaching. I first discovered her Medieval and Renaissance recorder and frame drum arrangements, while searching for quality, yet approachable, music for my elementary recorder consort.

During my Ph.D. studies, I focused on IMC's approach to recorder teaching, and her pure adherence to the Orff-Schulwerk philosophy, learned from the masters themselves. I wished I could travel back in time to learn under Isabel's tutelage, but through her letters and essays, I discovered IMC's commitment to Orff and Keetman's elemental methods. For IMC, they don't get lost in translation.

I'm honored to provide a foreword for this collection of Carley's thoughts, essays, and wisdom. I am excited for these new, yet tried-and-true treasures to reach the next generation of Orff-Schulwerk educators and students.

Karen Stafford
Union, Missouri

# ABOUT THE SCHULWERK

What, precisely, is the Schulwerk?

The word "Schulwerk," although not the standard German term (*Schularbeit*), plainly translates to "school works." Carl Orff used it as an umbrella designation for all the music education instruction created under his auspices; Orff-Schulwerk is often used in this sense today. Eventually, and in more precise contexts, "the Schulwerk" has become academic shorthand for the six great volumes of *Orff-Schulwerk: Musik für Kinder*, whether the original or in translated versions. Written totally in collaboration with Gunild Keetman, the Schulwerk set consists of five numbered volumes (I to V), plus the unnumbered *Paralipomena* (the erudite title is a theological Greek loanword meaning "things omitted" from previous text, in this case the earlier Schulwerk volumes). The five numbered books were published in German from 1950-1954; the last was not issued until 1966.

Naturally enough, when interest in Orff's educational ideas spread beyond German-speaking countries, translations of the Schulwerk were wanted. These were encouraged and assisted by Orff and

Keetman. By most lights, the best full version in English – but not the only version – is Margaret Murray's translation, issued from 1957-1966. An early Schulwerk enthusiast, she also founded the UK Orff Society. (An internet search caution: not to be confused with Margaret A. Murray, deceased in 1963, the noted Egyptologist, English folklorist, and writer on witchcraft.)

A significant caveat about the Murray edition of the Schulwerk: it is *not* a literal rendering of the contents of the German edition. This is actually made explicit on the title page: "English version *adapted* [emphasis added] by Margaret Murray." Her reworkings (for example, using English substitutes for German *volkslieder*) was entirely sanctioned and endorsed. As Orff himself commented: "... it was not a case merely of translation, but rather of a *new Schulwerk interpretation* [emphasis added] of the respective indigenous children's songs and rhymes." Nonetheless, particularly for Americans, the Murray version can be mildly off-putting. The text is set out in British English, with songs, rhymes, and cultural allusions that are far more familiar to a UK-bred readership.

Murray does retain the original German organizational structure in her *Orff-Schulwerk: Music for Children* volumes, namely:

Volume 1 – Pentatonic
Volume 2 – Major: Drone Bass Triads
Volume 3 – Major: Dominant and Subdominant Triads
Volume 4 – Minor: Drone Bass Triads
Volume 5 – Minor: Dominant and Subdominant Triads
Paralipomena (34 pieces for voice and various instruments).

(Schott Music, Mainz, Germany, the publisher of the German volumes, also publishes the Murray volumes.)

Technicalities of translation aside, it is essential to keep in mind what the Schulwerk is – and is not. This can head off possible confusion

for those newly introduced to Orff music education, as well as serving
as some helpful background information for the reader of this present
book. These are some key points to remember:

- The Schulwerk volumes contain dense and challenging
  music materials not well-suited for young children. It was
  never intended as a curriculum or instructional program for
  kindergarten and elementary school age students.
- The Schulwerk is not designed for self-instruction; rather, it
  demonstrates for teachers and students an educational
  approach that unifies movement, speech, singing, playing,
  and improvisation, with exercises and pieces that support
  and integrate all these elements.
- Gunild Keetman, co-founder of the Orff Approach, made
  immense and fundamental contributions. She had met Orff
  as a student at the Güntherschule in Munich, Germany.
  From 1928 on, she was a teacher at the school, wrote music
  for dance and accompanying instruments, and led the
  school orchestra for the Günther Dance Troupe. A decade
  younger than Orff, she collaborated with him in workshops
  and wrote instructional pieces for the early Orff-Schulwerk
  collection.
- The volumes of *Musik für Kinder* are not a significant
  departure from Orff and Keetman's earlier pedagogical
  works. Drawing on materials they prepared for their 1948-
  49 Bavarian school radio programs, the newly written
  volumes were seen as an extension, not a replacement, of
  the much earlier *Orff-Schulwerk: Elementare Musikübung*
  (Elementary Music Exercises). Also, these new volumes
  were not considered a final or concluding effort, as
  supplementary materials were added for another thirty
  years.
- Keetman's teaching pieces for xylophone, percussion, and
  recorder are important extensions of the Schulwerk; her

later books further expand the Orff repertoire and resources. For example, in *Elementaria: First Acquaintance with Orff-Schulwerk*, she clarifies the learning progression, and explains how best to teach it.

- Most Schulwerk pieces are not meant for young students; many parts are challenging to play even for teachers. Instead, these are model pieces for the Orff ensemble of recorders, xylophones, pitched and unpitched instruments, and other unconventional "instruments" like body percussion – claps, *patschen*, stamps, and snaps.
- Teachers are expected to simplify the Schulwerk pieces, write new original texts, and modify the instrumentation for their own classrooms.
- A *universal* version of the Schulwerk is not possible by definition. Orff believed that the Schulwerk was readily adaptable to other cultures and musical traditions, including non-Western ones. In more than thirty countries, each version is different, including the more recent American editions. The included folk songs in many languages are suited to each local culture, as are the rhymes and poems, but the underlying pedagogy is consistent. As a result, there is only one Orff Approach, but many delightful Schulwerks.

In IMC's own writings, she often discusses or refers to the Schulwerk (or Orff-Schulwerk), customarily referring to the Murray volumes. But occasionally, she is thinking of the more extensive literature that encompasses works by Keetman (cited in passim) and other materials drawn directly from the Schulwerk.

This expanded sense seems in line with Orff's own commentary that the Schulwerk "did not develop from any pre-considered plan – I could never have imagined such a far-reaching one." Besides the apparent structural problems, IMC was certainly aware of debatable flaws in both the Murray edition and German original, and she would recommend changes and alternatives for American Orff teachers and students.

Still, for over forty years, she never wavered in her admiration and support, confident that the Orff Approach made – and would continue to make – an inspired impact on education for children around the world.

Selected Related References

## Margaret Murray:

https://www.the-independent.com/news/people/news/margaret-murray-teacher-inspired-by-carl-orff-to-become-a-force-in-musical-education-in-britain-and-around-the-world-a83061.html

*Orff Re-Echoes: Selections From the Orff Echo & The Supplements*, Books 1 and 2, Edited by IMC (AOSA, 1977 and 1985)

*Music for Children: Orff-Schulwerk American Edition*, supervised by Hermann Regner of the Orff Institute (Schott Music), in three volumes:

> Volume 1 – Preschool
> Volume 2 – Primary
> Volume 3 – Secondary

## Orff and Keetman – brief biographical sketches:

http://aosa.org/about/orff-keetman/

## Carl Orff in performance (YouTube video) – *Astutuli* (1953):

https://www.youtube.com/watch?v=HogcJoRBiEw

# WHO WAS CARL ORFF?

Carl Orff was a 20th Century German composer (1895-1982), the creator of *Carmina Burana*, his celebrated 1937 cantata, performed to this day, and the founder of a music education method for children. You might read something like this in a general reference.

But that would provide no hint of either the unconventional aspects of his music or the truly innovative nature of the approach to music teaching he developed with Gunild Keetman. Nor does it convey anything of his curious mind, mostly good-humored disposition, and talent for creative collaboration. Plainly, more is needed to gain some insight into the life and career of this remarkable and remarkably flawed man.

Yet where to begin with Orff? First, even to categorize his musical style or educational thinking is not straightforward. While influences on him are traceable, he defies easy assignment to any school of classical music or to one of the modern music movements of his time. Similarly, his pedagogical ideas can only be aligned in a broad fashion with other progressive programs. Orff was determined to march to his own drummer – after he had seen to the design of the drum. (In fact, he collected, and commissioned, the pitched and unpitched percussion known today as "Orff instruments.")

Consider, then, a serious composer who puts significant effort into writing and arranging tunes for students. And seeks to integrate movement and speech with his music. And sets Medieval Latin poems and macaronic verses (Latin mixed with vernaculars like French or German), and later devises dramatic pieces in his version of his native Bavarian dialect. Plus, he scores for instruments unfamiliar or obsolete in the symphony orchestras of his day. He reexamines ancient scales and modes from before the age of Bach. He recasts a Monteverdi opera from the early 1600s and revives its vocal performance styles, yet explores rhythmic percussion, the "foundation of music," with an avant-garde sensibility. Lastly, imagine someone who wants to unite all these – music, dance, singing, acting, stage effects – into one grand experience. Someone who pictures a new spectacle, a totality inspired by the arts of the ancient Greek Muses, based on classical drama or folktales or fairy tales, yet fully alive to a 20th Century audience. Who would dare such a mad vision?

Carl Orff did.

Accordingly, he would spend a lifetime attempting to synthesize and realize his artistic dreams. Had his life not been overshadowed by Germany's history in the first half of the 20th Century – those brazen stumbles from one wrenching political period to another – he might well have found a more accommodating path and won renown for his music and educational projects with just his private lapses to atone for. But sadly, this is not the case.

He will live under four regimes: the German Empire, the Weimar Republic, Nazi Germany, and the West German *Bundesrepublik*. Like many others with comfortable backgrounds and education, he is indifferent to the fall of the Empire, ignores the slow collapse of open-minded Weimar, learns to kowtow in the frenetic and then nightmarish years of Hitler, and survives to be embraced – many years after World War II – by a free, democratic, and prosperous West Germany, a government of genuine stability and peace.

Back when Kaiser Wilhelm II rules, Orff is born in 1895 to a well-regarded military family in Munich. He is engrossed in music from the age of six, and, guided by his mother, a trained pianist, learns several instruments, although he is soon drawn to composing. After his studies at the Munich Academy of Music, he holds several theatrical positions and composes his first mature pieces in a variety of forms. Called up in 1917 for World War I military service and sent to the Eastern front, Orff almost dies when buried under collapsing rubble in a trench. Physically recovered, he's back in Munich at twenty-three, another restless soul the war has spit out.

The Allies defeat Germany, the Kaiser abdicates, and a miasma of political agitation and violent unrest envelops the country. But Orff has conceived his own personal salvation in a new music that he must bring to life. This "elemental music" will be attuned to ancient and modern sources, open to non-Western instruments and outside of the fusty traditionalism of academies, and intimately meshed with other arts, especially movement and dance. Orff believes he will have to study and experiment with everything. His friends at Munich University can help. The students at the new school he is co-founding will surely be eager participants. Then the best resulting instructional compositions and explanatory notes might be published in a series of books, alongside his own serious pieces for the concert hall and stage.

The new Güntherschule opens its doors in Munich in 1924. Orff is not yet thirty. The co-founder, Dorothee Günther (1896–1975), is a year younger, a dancer and choreographer with teaching credentials in physical education and gymnastics. She has conceived her all-girls school (ages 14-22) as a place for modern dance to unsettle the last vestiges of Victorianism. The curriculum must reject old forms and discover new ones, and reset the relationship of movement to music.

Günther wants to reawaken youthful idealism, and in Orff and teachers like Maja Lex, the dancer and budding choreographer, she has found kindred spirits for the school.

Professor Orff, the new director of the department of dance and music, has been a married man since 1920, already with an infant daughter. (He and his wife divorce a year after the school opens; he will marry three more times.) In the late 1920s, Orff is a quiet member of Munich's small but vibrant modernist circle that presents works by Schoenberg, Bartok, Hindemith, Stravinsky, and other notorious composers. Additionally, he conducts at the Munich Bach Club, a group dedicated to renewing appreciation of the master's repertoire.

Orff's star is on the rise. Publisher Schott Music has agreed to inaugurate a new series, *Orff-Schulwerk: Elementare Musikübung* ("Elementary Music Exercises"), starting with Orff's *Rhythmische-melodische Übung* ("Rhythmic-melodic Exercises"). This will be followed by more collaborative books and pamphlets issued from 1931 to 1934, now commonly referred to together as the "first Schulwerk."

Developed in school workshops led by Orff and his colleague and assistant Gunild Keetman (1904-1990), this first Schulwerk is intended for music teachers and advanced students. Another assistant, Hans Bergese, also contributes, while Keetman writes several instructional books, notably for recorder. Nearly a decade younger than Orff, Keetman is a steadfast admirer, a student at the school, and then a teacher from 1928 on. Besides working with Orff, she composes music for the dance classes and guides the school's orchestra, an integral component of the movement courses and the performances of the acclaimed Güntherschule dance troupe.

In these same years, Munich is Adolf Hitler's adopted home. The German economy continues to deteriorate in the worldwide Great Depression of the early 1930s. Far left and right political groups jockey viciously for power; the great dark Nazi tide is preparing to sweep over the nation. Having won outright control in 1934 – or rather, having hijacked the government – Hitler and his Nazi henchmen aim to totally reshape German society. They harass, degrade, and murder German Jews, purge dissidents and remaining opponents, appoint supporters at all levels of government bureaucracy, and proclaim that dissent will not be tolerated. Following decades of turmoil, the nation is calm at last – as quiet as the prison cell, the padded room, and the grave.

Around 1935, Orff seems to be equivocating like other disenchanted, loyal German citizens. He's not well known outside of Munich, but has a reputation as a composer, a former Kapellmeister, a writer, performer, director, and educator. His natural inclination is to disdain politicians, and he definitely prefers the rarified heights of serious music. He has chosen his friends and colleagues for their creative stimulation and intellectual abilities, and he is very much a part of artistic circles in Munich, even collaborating with his fellow Bavarian, Bertolt Brecht – a known Marxist – on a project. Orff also has many Jewish friends, including Kurt Weill and the poet Franz Werfel.

With that personal history, Orff is already frowned on by the new Munich authorities. Somehow he fails to disclose that one of his grandfathers was a Jewish convert to Catholicism; moreover, he has long been targeted by right-wing cultural critics as a leftist sympathizer, and denounced as a cultural bolshevist. Nonetheless, Orff apparently decides, as did Günther and Keetman, that they could ride out the political storm. They would comply. They would acquiesce to Nazi demands. And they would try to ingratiate themselves with important officials, a strategy to which Orff brought the most savvy and charisma.

For several years, the Güntherschule and its branch in Berlin continued to flourish. Faculty creative works for the 1936 Berlin

Olympics were well received at Hitler's triumphant showcase: Orff wrote festival songs; Gunild Keetman conducted the youth orchestra that played them (there's a phonograph recording); Dorothee Günther co-choreographed the immense, open-air dance spectacle performed by thousands of young girls and children. Although Germany was technically at peace, the military was rapidly rearming and propaganda for *Lebensraum* (literally, "living space") to justify the coming invasions was in full flower. Hitler would be named *Time* magazine's Man of the Year in 1938.

A year earlier, *Carmina Burana* was first produced. A contentious hit in 1937, it eventually became the most popular new concert music in Nazi Germany. Some influential Nazi music critics initially grumbled that neither the "primitive" style nor the composer was suitable for the Third Reich. But others disagreed, and popular appeal trumped the critics. Senior officials who knew next to nothing about music liked the big, thumping, drumming waves of sound. Orff was hailed; he now seemed on his way to bigger things.

A few words about *Carmina Burana*. The full Latin title is *Carmina Burana: Cantiones Profanae, Cantoribus et choris cantandae comitantibus instrumentis atque imaginibus magicis*. Or in English, "Poems of Beuren: Secular Songs for singers and choruses to be sung together with instruments and magic images." It's Orff's old dream, certainly, and he conceived his "scenic cantata" as a fully staged work with orchestra, dance movement, and visual stage effects. This is the "Theatrum Mundi" ("World Theater") that is ever close to his heart.

(Beuren is an area in Bavaria, Germany, and its Benediktbeuern Abbey is where the manuscript was found – the largest Latin songbook to survive from the Middle Ages. The full story of Orff's discovery and writing of the libretto, aided by Michel Hofmann, a Munich bureaucrat and Greek and Latin enthusiast, is even more convoluted, but there's no missing Orff's taste for showy intellectualism.)

The original poems are profane to a fault, ribald, luscious, and bawdy, with much devotion to love and drinking. The libretto's mixture of Latin, Middle High German, and a dash of French surely went right over the heads of casual audiences. A good thing, too, as these were not the "pure" Teutonic values the arts were supposed to be celebrating in Nazi Germany. Orff himself thought he had reached a high-water mark and wrote to his publisher: "Everything I have written to date ... can be destroyed. With *Carmina Burana* my collected works begin."

At the time of the premiere, he was forty-one, and could never have guessed that the self-proclaimed thousand-year Reich had only eight more years until its utter defeat. If Orff had managed to stay in the shadows and scrape by, he might have emerged from World War II with his reputation largely intact. But he was caught up in a Nazi-spun spider web. He likely thought they were a bunch of ill-educated dolts; but they were powerful spiders. And he was an artistic fly lured by promises of fame, position, and support for the Schulwerk. In the end, little was fulfilled, but in the pursuit, Orff deluded himself and misplaced his moral compass.

World War II begins in 1939. German armies are stunningly successful and the Nazi future looks bright. But perhaps in the general euphoria, Germans should have paid sobering heed to "O Fortuna," the text Orff chose to bookend *Carmina Burana*. That medieval poem lyrically exhorts the Wheel of Fortune: "O Fortune/like the moon/you are changeable...." Those who are brought to the heights by fate can be brought down to nothing when the wheel turns.

From 1942 on, the wheel is turning for Hitler's regime. The US joins the war after Pearl Harbor and the Allies – chiefly the US, Britain, and Russia (USSR) – are gearing up for a massive counterpunch. The war will be carried to Germany with extensive bombing raids.

The German military increasingly finds itself running near empty, slowly pressed back on the defensive.

In Munich, the Güntherschule's luck is also running out. Dorothee Günther has done everything to keep the school open, joining the Party and distancing the academic program from the Schulwerk. Orff is disaffected and loses interest; he seems to have withdrawn or been dismissed. Anyway, he is far more intent on his own officially sanctioned commissions and performances, as he is a figure on the national cultural stage. Then in 1944, the Nazis abruptly shut down the school. They need the building for a military depot.

An Allied air raid hits the building in early 1945. The teaching materials, musical instruments, costumes, and years of archives are still stored there, and all are destroyed. Only a few months later the war in Europe is over; Germany is defeated and surrenders in May, 1945. Hitler kills himself.

Like millions of other dazed Germans, Orff now finds himself on the wrong side of history. The Allied occupying force puts him on a provisional blacklist; he will be required to undergo a "denazification" interrogation. Orff reports for his interview. The Wheel of Fortune turns again.

His examiner is a US intelligence officer and former student of Orff's who remembers him fondly. (It seems he may actually have been on the lookout for his old teacher.) Orff talks his way, or is coached, into a clean report – it's disputed what exactly he claimed. But it was a plausible enough anti-Nazi cover story, especially to sympathetic American ears. Now fifty, Orff would be allowed to resume his career – and collect his *Carmina Burana* royalties.

He manages to scrounge by until another stroke of good fortune comes his way. In 1948, Bavarian Radio contacts him. They ask if he could do some broadcast music lessons for young school children. Jumping at the opportunity, Orff reconnects with Gunild Keetman.

He can use her help to recast the Schulwerk for this much younger audience.

The very first broadcast is "Die Weihnachtsgeschichte" ("The Christmas Story") with Orff's text and Keetman's music. It's a tremendous success. More broadcasts are set, featuring a group of German students playing recorders and Orff instruments to demonstrate the aural part of the modified Schulwerk program. After a year of these broadcasts, Orff and Keetman begin work on a new five-volume set, *Orff-Schulwerk: Musik für Kinder* ("Music for Children"). Schott Music, his old firm and another survivor of the war, will publish the volumes from 1950-1954, with a sixth added later.

For these new volumes, they compose and arrange folk tunes and original pieces for recorders, Orff instruments, and other standard instruments like the guitar. Keetman edits and revises materials from the first Schulwerk, since the considerably younger radio audience has opened up a new educational arena, but there are no fundamental pedagogical departures. It becomes the basis for the Orff Approach, gaining admirers in Germany and then in other countries. Margaret Murray raises the Orff banner in Britain; translations are underway. Within ten years, there is so much international interest that Orff and Keetman will take on lecture tours in Portugal, Canada, and Japan.

Orff went on with his work over another three decades, eventually producing some eighteen major works. *Carmina Burana* remains secure in the repertoire, and is among the most popular pieces of classical music ever composed. (It has won the high accolade of mass culture with its use in TV ads and movie soundtracks.) A new Orff-Institut building was inaugurated in 1963 in Salzburg, Austria; in 1972, the University of Munich awarded Orff an honorary doctorate. The West German government bestowed more honors, and the French gave him an award. Orff was now a grand old man of

German classical music, widely admired until his death in Munich in 1982.

As the war years faded, Orff and many other Germans fell into an awkward silence. No one wanted to remember. At best, Orff was an apolitical man caught up in terrible times who cooperated in order to survive; at worst, he willingly went along – although he never joined the Nazi party. His only daughter felt that he lived for music and only for music. Nonetheless, Orff had to know the Nazi era had grossly deformed his life and that he had turned his back on braver men, including his best friend who resisted, and Jewish colleagues who fled or were persecuted. But moral failures in other great artists have eventually been overlooked, and perhaps that should be the case with Carl Orff.

Better yet, think of him, say, in Toronto in 1962. Here he is inspiring a room full of American and Canadian music teachers with his dramatic declaiming. Never mind that he's orating in Bavarian dialect and probably no one understands, for he is so mesmerizing that he enthralls the audience, including the music teacher from Indianapolis who will write the essays in this book.* This is his Schulwerk legacy that stays forever unsullied: a call to teachers to naturally inspire their students to play and love music.

—

*J. Stryder is a writer and editor.*

---

\* For IMC's experience, see Chapter 18, "Improvisation Makes it Happen."

# INTRODUCTION & BIOGRAPHICAL NOTE

## Introduction: Bringing the Orff Approach to Life

Isabel McNeill Carley, my mother, strove to bring the Orff Approach to life. It supercharged her own professional life in 1962, when she attended the first-ever North American Orff-Schulwerk course in Toronto. IMC (the abbreviation of her full name used throughout this book) came away inspired. More than that, she was determined to learn more.

The next academic year (1963-64) she completed an intensive one-year course of study – in German – at the Orff-Institut in Salzburg, Austria, earning a Specialist's Diploma with Honors. She also studied composition privately with Carl Orff, the composer who had, with his longtime colleague Gunild Keetman, devised the Orff Approach. Once credentialed, IMC went about spreading the word, every way she knew how.

This posthumous collection of essays, sketches, and notes – and even a children's story to be read aloud – is a memorial to the breadth of her interests and the passion she brought to advocating for music education. I hope the headnotes I have provided at the beginning of each chapter provide a sense of IMC's personality and commitment to her work.

As one of her students, and for a time a fellow teacher of Orff pedagogy, I thought I understood her professional narrative. Then, as executor of her literary estate, I discovered more early unpublished materials bearing witness to the same dedication. For example, in graduate school during the early days of US involvement in World War II, she wrote of her fervent belief in the power of childhood education to change the future. She never abandoned that belief.

If anything, the Orff Approach appealed to her because it served the same educational vision. In a similar way, when brain science was changing our language and popularizing the Left-brain/Right-brain view of personhood, IMC latched on to that information. She remained fascinated by science, art, and literature that explored theory as well as practice, all toward one purpose: build a better way to reach people – especially children – with music, speech, and movement. Bring them all into the circle; let everyone participate, invent, and enjoy. As she put it, "The emphasis is on playing with the materials of music, on developing musical ideas just as a composer does." In her view, *everyone* has a place inside that circle.

One fundamental lesson she brought home from the Orff Institute was the crucial importance of discovering North American traditional music, songs, rhymes, and stories for use in the American classroom. Appreciating immediately the great pedagogic value in the Schulwerk of gapped pentatonic scales, she wanted more. She realized that the five German Schulwerk volumes – and the folk traditions they drew from – were actually deficient in the vast melodic and tonal riches of the pentatonic modes. In all her subsequent teaching and writing, she spread the word that our homegrown folk materials surpassed in subtlety and soulfulness what the German-language Schulwerk sources had to offer.

IMC recognized that *incompleteness* is a necessary feature of the Orff teacher's career. Once embarked on their own improvisatory quests, these teachers know they can never arrive. Always in motion, they open wide the circle to all their students, welcoming them to the lifelong joys of confident, secure music making.

It's a challenging life to choose. IMC committed to that life wholeheartedly, and influenced many others to make the same generous, demanding choice.

## Biographical Note

Gunild Keetman, IMC, Carl Orff, Liselotte Orff in Salzburg, Austria, 1963-64

Isabel McNeill Carley was one of the co-founders of the American Orff-Schulwerk Association (AOSA). She served on the AOSA Board, edited *The Orff Echo* magazine for its first fifteen years (1968-1983), and contributed to the AOSA task forces on Recorder and Curriculum in the 1990s. In recognition, AOSA established the Isabel McNeill Carley Library and honored her with the AOSA Distinguished Service Award.

For sixty years, she devoted herself to her work as a music educator and composer. A leader of Orff certification courses in the United States, she taught workshops for AOSA chapters and Title III programs, participated in national and state-level Music Educators National Conference (MENC, now NAfME) events, led trainings in Europe and Asia, and presented sessions at national and regional AOSA conferences. Throughout her long working life, she taught music privately and in school settings, both to children and adults.

As a performing musician, IMC sang alto, and played recorders, keyboards, and percussion. She also wrote arrangements of works from the Medieval and Renaissance instrumental repertoire. Her numerous published works include compositions for recorders, Orff ensemble, piano, voice, and percussion. (See "IMC Selected Bibliography" in the back matter for details.)

Born in 1918, she grew up in Toronto and Chicago, returned to Chicago for graduate school, and married James Carley there in 1943. After ten years in the Western US, and now the parents of three, they moved to Indianapolis, Indiana. He was a professor of sacred music at Christian Theological Seminary and she built her music teaching, performing, and composing career. Twenty years later, they moved to the mountains of Western North Carolina where they spent another thirty years together. Isabel retired from active teaching in 2004, and the couple made a final move to Maryland, where James died in 2006 and she in 2011.

—

*Anne M Carley is a creativity coach, editor, and writer based in Charlottesville, VA. She manages Brasstown Press, publisher of this and other books by Isabel McNeill Carley.*

# THE PENTATONIC SCALE

## ANNE M CARLEY

C Pentatonic Scale

*Pentatonic is not synonymous with easy.* — IMC

The gapped pentatonic scale is a thing of beauty. So IMC believed, and so she built her pedagogic apparatus. Along with improvisation, this was one of her favorite aspects of the entire Orff Approach.

Why take away notes from the major and minor scales we know and love? Because when you remove notes (typically the half-steps, like F and B in a C scale), the notes that are left are consonant together. In other words, when you play those remaining notes in combinations of your choosing, you are almost guaranteed to sound good. Other players using the same scale will sound musical together. Add a skilled teacher to make cogent suggestions and provide a steady beat, and you'll have budding musicians all over the room.

Improvisation?

No problem. It's going to sound just fine.

Technically, pentatonic can mean any five-note scale within the span of an octave. Pentatonic does not refer only to the gapped scales sans half steps; though in the Orff Approach, that's the usual meaning. Using the familiar barred "Orff Instruments" – xylophone, glockenspiel, metallophone – you can take advantage of the removable bars to create numerous pentatonic scales.

As IMC liked to point out, "Pentatonic is not synonymous with easy." Often underestimated by composers and academics, the gapped scales lend themselves to subtle and magical lines, moods, and harmonies. These open scales aren't boring, either. By shifting the "home" note within one pentatonic scale, the adventurer can embrace a variety of the pentatonic modes: gapped scales built not only on *Do*, but also on *Re*, *Mi*, *So*, and *La*.

Each tonal center brings its own personality to the music you make in its realm. Folk traditions – many of them in North America – celebrate the space for ambiguity and depth that only gapped pentatonic scales and modes offer.

Those half steps that create tension in the familiar music we hear everywhere in the Western world – a magnetic pull that draws our ears (and brains) toward a predetermined tonality – are simply missing. When these tension-producing half steps are removed, the result is a more inviting and open-ended musical environment.

It is a realm full of possibilities for everyone, child or adult. As a safe place to begin playing and improvising, the pentatonic scale is ideal. Before moving on to the full diatonic scale, half steps and all, fortunate is the student who first dwells in the sonic valley of the pentatonic. Confidence and imagination thrive there.

In honor of the power of the pentatonic, we have organized the essays in this book into sections, each one named for a note in the C Pentatonic scale.

—

*For more on the musical theory behind the pentatonic scale, see "Pentatonic Scales and Modes" herein and also IMC's essay, "The Musical Realm of the Pentatonic," in* Making It Up As You Go, *from Brasstown Press.*

# TAKING THE ORFF APPROACH TO HEART

*For the first time in pedagogical history,
there is a form of music education from
the composer's point of view, with the
focus on early ensemble experience as
the basis for lifelong delight in music making.*

ISABEL MCNEILL CARLEY

# PART 1

## CREATIVE CLASSROOMS FOR CHILDREN

**C**

## Middle C

## *Do*

[waist level]

# CREATIVE CLASSROOMS FOR CHILDREN

*Anything is understood only to the extent that it is reinvented.*

JEAN PIAGET

# 1 THE CASE FOR CREATIVITY

*IMC loved those moments when a student – child or adult – surprised everyone.*

The impact of creative work in the classroom cannot be measured. You may never know when you strike fire, when a particular child finds himself musically for the first time. Children are too inarticulate to tell us; and they may not even know themselves for years. A class period that disappoints you may be, for some child, the most important of all her days in school. It is easy to misjudge what we are really accomplishing or when our students are really learning in our classes. It is too easy to fall back on the old and obvious standards: "How many songs did they learn this year?" and "How well did they perform?"

Of course, children should perform when they're ready or when they want to share what they've been learning. But perfecting and performing set pieces is only a small part of the Orff Approach. It is much too easy to succumb to public pressure for too frequent performances, or to buff our own professional ambition and vanity by using selected, talented students to build our reputations. That's a travesty of the Schulwerk, a complete denial of its underlying philosophy.

What do you remember of your school music classes? Vividly, with real pleasure? The one day – out of all my years of music classes – that stands out in my memory is when Miss McKay let our fifth grade class compose our own tune to Longfellow's poem, "The Children's Hour." (A curious choice it seems to me now.) She read the entire poem, then lined it out and asked for volunteers to sing each phrase. By the end of the class, we had a made a wholly new song, to our credit. But the class exercise was a shot in the dark, and never happened again. Probably it wasn't much of a tune, but one of the phrases in it was mine. It was the first time in my life that anyone had suggested – much less allowed – that I could make music of my own. Yet all the while I had been taking piano lessons for five years and going to music classes, three days a week, for three years.

The situation is little better today. There is still confusion over what is meant by creativity. "Creative activities" may be scheduled in many classrooms, but do they actually spark creative thought? Or are they done merely for appearance's sake and because the current text-book suggests "do a creative project" that amounts to little more than learning a song or listening to a recording.

There is far more to it that that! This superficial use of creative projects does more harm than good, since it denies the basic serious-ness of the task. There must be a definite musical problem with defi-nite limits, and for which preparatory training in improvisation has been completed so that the children can be allowed to solve it almost entirely on their own. Help and guidance should be on call if students ask for it, but when improvisation is actually going on there must be no criticism by the teacher. Peer judgments afterwards bear far more weight; there is less danger of discouragement if the teacher's judgment is reserved till after the creative work is finished.

Nowadays there is so much academic pressure at the high school and college levels that many gifted young people must forego their musical interests. It becomes all the more important to make music classes in elementary school so alive and meaningful that their participants will keep coming back to playing music all their lives. In the best cases, they'll recall a growing sense of their own creative ability to make music with others. Perhaps they will remember years later, not one isolated day, but day after shining day of discovery and achievement.

—

*A version of this essay first appeared in The Orff Echo Volume 2 Issue 1 (published as Volume 1 Issue 4) [November 1969]. Reprinted with permission from The Orff Echo, the quarterly journal published by the American Orff-Schulwerk Association.*

## 2  THAT LOVELY TWO-HEADED BETSY HIGGINBOTTAM

*As new brain research emerged in the 1960s and 70s, IMC read about it voraciously, excited to integrate the new theories with her experience as an educator. Subsequent decades of research have refined the simplistic mapping IMC refers to here, yet her vision of a unified, balanced approach to life and creativity remains vivid.*

Judy Thomas

*Illustration © Judith A Thomas. Used with permission.*

Years ago I enjoyed reading a garbled account of a social occasion in a small Midwestern town. Reprinted as a short squib in *The New Yorker*, as I recall, it described in detail two hats worn by a Betsy Higginbottam to the same event. For some reason, I latched onto a silly mental picture: a lady with two enormous hats on her head at once. The image has stayed in my mind all these years, and surfaced again as I read recent reports about our dual brains.

It is only in the last ten years that researchers have learned that each of us has, in effect, two brains inside our heads. These two brains have very different abilities and assignments. In most of us, the left hemisphere is dominant. It is the side of the brain that handles speech and visual imagery, and controls the muscles of the right half of the body. The brain's right hemisphere, on the other hand, is the seat of spatial, musical, intuitive, and creative abilities, controlling the muscles of the left half of the body.

Our rational abilities dominate in our left hemispheres. This is the side on which education in the Western tradition has concentrated. All the recent upheavals in education in our country – student unrest, the insistence on "relevance," the establishment of alternative schools, free universities, etc. – seem to me symptomatic of a developing awareness of the inadequacies of the old curricula. These are programs based on verbal, logical, left-brain abilities. Students and educators alike are protesting that this isn't enough.

In a period of rapid change like ours, we need more than this. We need to learn to educate the whole person. We need to find new ways of integrating personality, using all the abilities we human beings possess. We need to learn to educate our emotions to foster cooperation rather than competition. We need to cultivate flexibility and to teach improvisation. In an age in which facts become obsolete so fast, and jobs become outmoded, the ability to improvise and to find new solutions becomes all-important.

Clearly it is through the arts that this other, different kind of learning is most readily accessible. If we as music teachers accept these findings of our foremost psychologists, there are, it seems to me, some rather obvious changes to be made in music education:

If musical ability is nonverbal, seated in the right half of the brain, then we must approach it on a nonverbal level.

If nonverbal, then music is allied with right brain movement abilities, and it must be approached through movement.

Verbalization, logical thought, analysis, and theory should come AFTER years of participation in music. These rhythmic and intuitive musical powers should be developed at the stage when a child's new analytical powers are just beginning to grow. There is always an optimum time for any human learning.

Anticipating or delaying it will defeat the purpose, make learning tedious and difficult for the child. According to Piaget, children learn best through active, direct manipulation of their materials, not through external instruction. Verbal understanding develops gradually, and only after much sensorimotor activity. The teacher's job is not to transmit information or concepts alone, but to give the child the opportunity to *act* on both a physical and abstract level.

As skill in abstraction, verbalization, etc. develops, music affords a unique opportunity to combine the rational and intuitive abilities of human beings in cooperative endeavors. The individual contributes an essential part to the whole, and that helps to produce more than could ever be done alone.

Music as art speaks to and from our deepest levels of consciousness; as a skill, it involves our highest mental faculties. Where it is taught on both levels, each at the proper time in human development, it affords the most humanizing core curriculum available to human beings. Music can unite in one discipline both hemispheres of our brains, providing the basis for a new synthesis in Western education.

The Orff Approach, with its emphasis on participation, on ensemble, on movement, and on improvisation best reflects and applies these new findings of our most advanced psychologists. It affords a wealth of sensorimotor experience as a basis for later visual and verbal skills; for as in language development, sound comes before the use of sight. With this basis in actually making music, understanding and enjoyment grow from childhood on, and lead to whatever level or style of music making or music appreciation the individual can reach. The foundation for a dual mind unified in lifelong balance has been laid.

—

*A version of this essay first appeared in The Orff Echo Volume 8 Issue 1 [September 1975]. Reprinted with permission from The Orff Echo, the quarterly journal published by the American Orff-Schulwerk Association.*

# 3   CREATE OR PERFORM

*In music education IMC was a fierce advocate of the process, rather than the performance. Although she is sympathetic to the enormous pressures on music teachers to wow their audiences, IMC urges teachers to resist and rethink.*

In recent years, many speeches, articles, books, and several large-scale government projects have promoted creativity in the arts. There remains a lot of misunderstanding among parents, school administrators, and music teachers themselves as to the value and practicality of creative work in the school music class. The battle was won a generation ago in teaching visual art, so that children today are trusted to use their own eyes and taste, no matter how strange the results may appear to adults. When art skills are allowed to develop gradually, an appreciation of the world's artistic heritage can arrive over time.

Creativity in music is much more of a problem. Music by its nature can never be a totally private undertaking. Experimentation with sound and movement should have place in class instruction before serious group music making is attempted. This takes time and patience, and careful planning. It also takes a certain attitude on the part of the teacher, as nothing genuinely creative can emerge from an atmosphere that is tense, critical, or impatient.

In all the writing on the subject of creativity in education I have seen, the role of the teacher's personality has rarely been discussed, except in an old book by Rudolf Steiner. He explains the influence on children of different personality types, and even predicts the type of chronic physical ills that will afflict pupils in middle age as a result of their teachers' personalities! Perhaps he goes too far, but unquestionably he has a point. Nothing can grow to healthy maturity in an unhealthy climate. The climate of the classroom is the teacher's doing. Is it a place where a child can grow? Or does the teacher simply play it safe and do what he or she thinks is required?

This is a real problem for those aspiring to teach the Orff Approach. We are expected to provide musical entertainment for school groups at the drop of a hat, and at least in my town, for any civic group that invites us. The pressure is enormous, and it is easy to forget Orff's basic tenet that participation is more important than performance. If we do forget, we are cheating the children and betraying the inclusive humanizing spirit of the whole approach.

I will concede it is better for children to be pushed into perfecting and performing Orff arrangements, designed by one of the great composers of our day, than to prepare a more conventional concert. Those who are selected undoubtedly gain in musical understanding, and the rhythmic training and ensemble experience are invaluable. But what of the ones who are rejected? What musical training do they get? It's the old story of exploiting the good kids and excluding everyone else. Is this education?

But, and a very large "but" it is, a performance is not the goal. It is all too easy for those of us brought up with this false emphasis to fall back into old habits. When we are on the spot and our whole career is open to public censure – as it is every time we perform or allow our classes to perform – of course we want the result to do us credit. Do we force our ideas on the children, or do we use theirs? Do we stick to the printed repertoire or adjust it to our own situation? Do we work out new ideas with our pupils and use those ideas in our public appearances? Do we trust them enough to ask them to improvise in public?

The need to create is basic and universal. To deny it is to frustrate the children entrusted to us. Surely there is enough adult-imposed pressure in the rest of the curriculum nowadays, without carrying into our music programs. It's our society's false standards: music is entertainment and the goal of music education is public performance. The human need to make something of our own and the power of music are denied in this narrow view. Every human being needs some kind of creative outlet. Failing to find this outlet results in frustration and aggression. As Erich Fromm said: "Violence is the outcome of the unlived life. The only answer is creativity."

Other cultures and civilizations have taken music much more seriously as a means of education. For the Greeks, it was central, embracing as it did the arts of poetry, drama, and dance. Plato said, "Rhythm and harmony penetrate very deeply to the inward places of the soul, and affect it most powerfully, imparting grace."

It is this recognition of the basic humanizing value of music that the Orff Approach regains. The goal is not the cultivation of technical skills, but the cultivation of imagination, of taste, of understanding, and of sensitivity. What other subject in the curriculum can do as much?

—

*This essay is reprinted from* Making It Up As You Go: Selected Essays, *Brasstown Press. Portions of this essay first appeared in The*

*Orff Echo Volume 1 Issue 2 [February 1969] and Volume 6 Issue 1 [November 1973]. These portions are reprinted with permission from The Orff Echo, the quarterly journal published by the American Orff-Schulwerk Association.*

# 4  MUSIC PLUS

## FIVE- AND SIX-YEAR-OLDS IN THE CLASSROOM

*In her manuscript for* Music Plus, *IMC designed an approach specifically for classroom teachers of kindergarten and first grade. She realized how much can be accomplished through the wise combination of movement, speech play, and music for very young children in what she termed a "cyclical-accretive" curriculum. Her lessons circle back reassuringly, while adding new layers of interest.Though her publisher successfully field-tested the book, it was never published. This essay is drawn from her introductory remarks for the classroom teacher.*

Music itself is made up of repetition and contrast, and so is the curriculum in this book. Little children need a great deal of repetition because it's only when they know material thoroughly that they can really enjoy it. Yet, like the rest of us, they also feel a need for variety and change, for transformations that are the educational equivalent of music's own contrasts.

Both repetition and transformation are built in to the movement exercises, rhymes, traditional sayings, stories, songs, and singing games I have included here. These materials are developed a little at a time, so there is a continuous process of growth by accretion throughout. But it is only rarely that anything is repeated in exactly the same way, and then only because the repetition is critical for young children trying to memorize something new.

*Music Plus* is so titled to make clear the multiple strands in the teaching of music to young children in kindergarten and first grade. Its nine units are divided into separate lessons, and each lesson is divided into three tracks: Movement, Speech Play, and Music.

All three are essential to each lesson, though it may be tempting to scant the areas you are least comfortable with yourself. The three tracks reinforce each other, and as the year goes on, the tracks overlap more and more; it becomes educationally arbitrary to which category a particular track activity is assigned.

Variety is built into the lesson structure with the Movement, Speech Play, and Music. New materials, new combinations, new concepts, and new emphases appear in each succeeding lesson. Sometimes this is simply a matter of novelty, as when new rhymes or songs are introduced; sometimes it's a fresh development of something learned earlier. Both are essential if children are to be kept involved and learning at their maximum capacity.

What began as a body percussion exercise may develop into a piece for unpitched percussion. That may lead to a dance that can be used in a dramatic situation. Or a rhyme may be developed into a song. And the song needs simple ostinato accompaniments on a xylophone, plus appropriate unpitched percussion instruments. Then new verses may be added which require dramatic play.

Improvisation is the essential creative activity – in movement, speech play, singing, rhythm drumming, and instrument playing. Here it is introduced as soon as there is even a minimum vocabulary to work with. It is rhythm that ties the whole classroom enterprise together and gives vitality and immediacy to every activity. There are always new possibilities to be explored in all the time allowed.

As Orff said, "All song must come from speech." Music has always developed in relation to speech, movement, and dance. It took our ancestors thousands of years to develop our present mathematical system of notating music. As the teacher, you should let young children have plenty of time to experience speech play, movement, body percussion play, using rhythm instruments, etc. before ever introducing music notation.

Even at this initial stage of Orff instruction, the emphasis is on playing with the materials of music, on developing musical ideas just as a composer does. In that way, music comes alive to children as an immediate and stimulating activity. Their participation and their own ideas are always being explored and developed. That is why it's so important to include real choices for the students – and for the teacher, too. The cultivation of artistic taste over time depends on us learning to make our own choices.

*Music Plus* is designed for kindergarten and first grade teachers who are with their students throughout the school day. The experienced teacher will discern that the lessons do have an underlying logical progression that is carefully considered; a scaffold for learning music, not a straitjacket. Student curiosity, the process of enrichment and extension, and the cultivation of language and movement skills in relation to rhythmic play are all more important than pedagogical box checking.

As far as I know, this book represents the first effort to combine movement, speech play, and music into a coherent curriculum appropriate for either classroom teachers or music specialists. It is what I choose to call a "cyclical-accretive" lesson plan. Rather than a standard, formulaic progression, I have tried to *cycle* through key activities, repeating them from lesson to lesson, while each time *accreting* (that is, adding on) some new knowledge or variation that advances the child's musical understanding. This is, when successfully carried out, the way for students to learn naturally. They absorb information seemingly by osmosis, because nothing has been forced, or coerced, or pressured.

Happily, students of any age can attain the stage of playing creatively with the materials of music. But only when they're fully comfortable with the materials, the assignment, and the class environment. That's been my own experience, a lifelong confirmation of all that I took to heart from the Orff Approach.

Now it is up to you to read and engage with what I hope is the most vibrant, the most challenging, the most comprehensive, and the most practical Orff Approach curriculum yet proposed.

—

*This essay was previously unpublished.*

# PART 2

## DELIGHTFUL DOINGS FROM DAY ONE

**D**

*Re*

# DELIGHTFUL DOINGS FROM DAY ONE

*Even at this initial stage of Orff instruction, the emphasis is on playing with the materials of music.*

ISABEL MCNEILL CARLEY

# 5  PLAYING WITH OUR MATERIALS: SPEECH PLAY

*IMC's expressive use of speech play in her own teaching sessions demonstrated its power to many. She understood its fundamental importance to the Orff Approach. As she says here, "Speech Play, Body Percussion, and Movement must necessarily come first in any Orff curriculum."*

Speech, of all our resources, is the most malleable. None of us will speak the same sentence – or adage, rhyme, or poem – exactly the same way. Think of all the variables: pitch, voice quality, inflection, tempo, emphasis, rhythm, and dynamics. They are never the same.

When we teach Orff music classes, the spoken word is the most appropriate way to introduce our students to improvisation, even for the youngest children, as there are vast untapped possibilities in the simplest of rhymes. Speech Play, the formal term for these verbal exercises, is far more important in children's musical development than most realize. It can provide the first guided, systematic exposure to rhythmic and expressive sounds. Think also of folk tales and nursery rhymes and songs that have been orally transmitted for generations. Like other heritage resources, the rhythm, tempo, vocal color, and range are determined only by the words themselves. With no set meter, there is an inherent fluidity and flexibility that is lost when the meter is predetermined.

For several centuries in Western culture, only inexact metrical notation was attached to song texts; it took still longer before our mathematically precise signs and symbols fully developed. Now the signs for rhythm and meter are independent of spoken language, but our ancestors took a thousand years to make the transition from the free rhythmic speech of ancient poetry and drama to the strictness of our current notation. A backward glance at history is also a good reminder: we should take our time before we guide our students into that mind-numbing world of notated music.

Let us also recall that normal human speech has a limited vocal range: the main "reciting tone" in which most of our conversation takes place; a somewhat higher range for emphasis; and a slightly lower range for less significant, private, or parenthetical communication. (Exaggerating this vocal range sounds false and phony.) Yet meaningful speech requires a musical line – just like a song – and a flowing rhythm. Since there is no single right way to say something pleasing to the ear, we have endless opportunities for variation and improvisation.

Speech Play is a solid, practical bridge to music training. Speech is something we humans cannot outgrow. Speech involves long and short syllables, accent, duple, triple, and compound meters, timbre, tempo, dynamics, and variable pitch – all these rudiments exist in music and can be explored first through Speech Play. In a repertoire of sayings, rhymes, and stories from our cultural traditions, we have a treasured basis for later musical development. Furthermore, it's fun. The children love it – and they learn to speak and to listen to others with new alertness.

Speech Play in the Schulwerk Volumes

I should note that in the Schulwerk, the whole section on Speech Play and Rhythmic Training is seemingly misplaced in the middle of Volume I. There are only a few speech exercises included in the first volume (in the Margaret Murray UK edition) – and all are translated from German texts or unfamiliar British substitutes. (Yes, we need to find our own American rhymes, poems, folk tales, and stories to supplement these obscure English nursery rhymes and stories.) Additionally, most of the songs and instrumental pieces in Volume I were not designed for beginning children, but were arranged for older students in Keetman's demonstration classes on the Bavarian radio programs. Orff and Keetman had to put these pieces together hurriedly, transferring ideas they had actually developed with their much older Güntherschule students years earlier.

As a result of what amounts to a historical misstep, too many of us assume incorrectly that we should begin with Schulwerk Volume I, Part I. This neglects the necessary training in Part II, which, pedagogically, should certainly come first. Because the educational progression is not clear in Volume I, we teachers must work to fill in the gaps and provide that essential basic training.

You'll find considerable help in Keetman's invaluable *Elementaria*. She spells out the correct progression in great detail. So does Brigitte Warner in her thorough and practical *Orff-Schulwerk: Applications for the Classroom*, a thoughtful guide to effective Orff teaching. (Schott publishes both books.) Also, the Keetman series of small gray books for xylophones is carefully sequenced from the easiest exercises onward.

Putting the Schulwerk's tangled order aside, Speech Play, Body Percussion, and Movement must necessarily come first in any Orff curriculum. These ought to be front and center in any teacher's lesson plan.

Speech Play Exercises for Young Children (K-2)

In the Schulwerk, the basic principles of rhythm and meter are taught by Speech Play, progressing from single words to rhythmic phrases to challenging exercises based on sayings, rhymes, short poems, folk tales, and stories. For the youngest children, first try "single word" exercises.

I like to start with name play. Choose four children whose names have different rhythms, for example: David, Eleanor, Mary Helen, and John. The chosen four stand in front of the class. I stand behind them and tap their heads lightly as the class says the name of whomever I tapped. I use an obvious rhythmic sequence first, (for example, David, Mary Helen, Eleanor, John) but later I will repeat (John, Eleanor, Eleanor, John with a triplet feel on Eleanor) or skip around (for example, Mary Helen, Mary Helen, David, John) to make more varied and complicated patterns with my taps.

A student volunteer or two next take a turn as the tapper. Then we choose another set of names. You can, of course, have students drum the same patterns on unpitched percussion, once the names can be used as beat cues. Or have the class work out "name dances" if you choose. (If you are lucky to have two students with contrasting double names, you can have two different steps on a name and extend the dance.) The name game works just as well using four fish, dogs, flowers, trees, dinosaurs, or anything else your class is currently interested in – but be sure the names have complementary beats.

Young children will greatly benefit from drills on steady beats and regular rhythms. Use Speech Play with lots of traditional rhymes, as many in the class will already know them. E.g., "One, two, tie my shoe" or "Hot Cross Buns" or "Bow, wow, wow, Whose dog art thou?" Start by saying and clapping the beat. Or walk to the beat as everyone says the rhyme together. Later, add supporting body percussion patterns to reinforce the rhythm. Keep the Speech Play easy, so every child can be successful. For example, have the children try patsching L R L R (left, right, left, right) on their knees for a lengthy interval before speaking the rhyme.

Introduce *patsch*-clap patterns as soon as the children seem ready. Then, before trying *stamp*-clap patterns, do marching rhymes to help them feel the beat in their feet. (Finger *snaps* can be left until a later time.)

Here are some good rhymes for marching:

> March, March
> *March, march, two by two,*
> *Dressed in yel – low, red and blue.*
> *March, march, three by three,*
> *Ma – ry, Bil – ly, march with me.*

> Two, Four, Six, Eight
> *Two, four, six, eight,*
> *Meet me at the garden gate.*
> *If I'm late, do not wait.*
> *Two, four, six, eight.*

> The King of France – *in duple time*
> *The King of France*
> *And forty thousand men*
> *Marched up hill,*
> *And then marched down again.*
> *And when they were up they were up,*
> *And when they were down they were down,*
> *And when they were only half way up*
> *They were neither up nor down.*

Higgledy, Piggledy, My Black Hen - *in 6/8*
*Higgledy, piggledy, my black hen,*
*She lays eggs for gentlemen,*
*Gentlemen come every day*
*To see what my black hen doth lay.*

Young children also need to experience many free rhythms. Use the rhymes and poems that hint at built-in promptings for improvisation and development. For example:

Intry, Mintry
*Intry, mintry, tribbledy fig,*
*Deema, dima, doma, dig,*
*Howchy, powchy,*
*Noma, nowchy,*
*Hum, tum, too,*
*Olliga, bolliga, boo,*
*Out ... goes ... YOU!*

Young children also enjoy John Ciardi's "If I could go as high and low..." here.

One of the delights of Speech Play is the rich vocal paraphony (defined in the glossary) that results when everyone speaks in his or her own natural range, with no attempt to match pitch. But first the class must agree on a common rhythm and inflection, so that the rhythm, voices, and "tune" are in sync. I love to use this nonsense rhyme, *Ungai, Mungai,* with K-2 classes, especially around Halloween:

> *Ungai, mungai,*
> *Alligator ungai,*
> *Chicka-chacka chungai,*
> *Over!*

("Ungai," "mungai," and "chungai" rhyme with FUN-guy.)

Take the time to explore the possibilities of the long, slow nonsense syllables as you lead the class with your voice and gestures. Then make it clipped and playful, with rests inserted between the words. Or extend it by making up other nonsense lines to rhyme with "Alligator ungai."

When the rhyme's familiar to the class, use it for a ball-bouncing game. Gather in a circle and bounce the ball in turn to each child while everyone says the rhyme. Later, bounce it erratically, to the children who are alert and ready to bounce it back. Some children can soon take turns as the leader while everyone chants. If it proves a favorite, let the class work out their own two or three note tune on A-G-E. Add body percussion, unpitched percussion, and/or a simple bordun on Bass Xylophone for the "orchestra" to play, while the singing children play the game.

*Ungai, Mungai*, with its long UNG syllables, affords endless possibilities for rhythmic Speech Play. Try any of the variations in this expanded list:

    a. Use it for echo-play, chanting very slowly, making good use of all the long *ung's*.

    b. Chant matter-of-factly, quite metrically, with body percussion accompaniment.

    c. Insert rests between the words, with a gradual crescendo.

    d. Repeat (c) in canon form with two groups.

    e. Change the meter to make it fast and playful.

  f. Make up a hand-sign tune using two or three notes the class knows, and use the class tune during the ball game.

  g. Add bar instrument and percussion accompaniment.

  h. Let volunteers work out movement to match the tune.

  i. Have a few recorder players alternate with the singers in playing the class tune.

  j. Put all the elements together – tune, movement, accompaniment – for a holiday celebration. Or just for fun!

DON'T try to do it all at once! It takes weeks of delighted play to find what your particular class most enjoys doing with it. And, of course, it would come out quite differently with each class, though the basic development would remain the same, from simple speech play to accompanied song and movement.

Let me suggest that you start immediately to make your own collection of rhymes and short poems that have some magic in them and suggest and deserve the same sort of extended play. (See resources in Chapter 6.)

A favorite of mine for primaries is the English rhyme, Christmas Pudding:

> *Into the pudding put the plums,*
> *Stirabout, stirabout, stirabout;*
> *Next , the good white flour comes,*
> *Stirabout, stirabout, stirabout..*
> *Sugar, and peel, and eggs, and spice,*
> *Stirabout, stirabout, stirabout;*
> *Mix them and fix them and bake them twice,*
> *Stir about, stir about, and stir about.*
> *Into the oven to bake all day,*
> *Riseabit, riseabit, riseabit.*
> *Out of the oven, and put it away,*
> *Wrap it, and pack it, till Christmas day!*

The children sit close together in one large circle (or two if the class is large) and pretend they've formed an enormous mixing bowl! They mime adding each ingredient to the pudding one by one, stirring them vigorously with imaginary wooden spoons, then wrapping and storing them. (The last two lines are mine, since the puddings can't stay in the oven indefinitely!)

Some traditional rhymes invite development into longer stories: Jack and Jill, Humpty Dumpty, Doctor Foster [British], Three Little Kittens, Little Miss Muffet.

One year I worked out a story for my preschoolers about Humpty Dumpty: Did you know that he lived in the little valley at the entrance to the royal palace with his egg-people friends? And that they all loved rolling on the green grass on the gentle hill in front of the royal gate? Humpty Dumpty, who was a born show-off, was particularly skillful. He liked to roll down quite fast and turn back up the hill until he reached the low end of the palace wall. Then he would roll cautiously and slower up the rising wall until he proudly perched high above the big gate. But one fine day, the royal coach suddenly came rushing and clattering up to the gate, with trumpets blaring while all the egg people rolled out of the way — all, that is, but Humpty Dumpty, who, in his excitement, fell off the wall right beside the drive, just as the king and all his men swung into the final curve....And you know the rest...

Here is a less familiar rhyme that supports dramatic play:

> *Father and Mother and Uncle John*
> *Went to the market one by one;*
> *Father fell off,*
> *Mother fell off,*
> *But Uncle John went on and on,*
> *and on and on, and on and on ...*

My five- and six-year-olds had fun deciding why Father, Mother, and Uncle John were going to market in the first place, and what they were taking. How did Father and Mother happen to fall from whatever they were riding on or in? How did Uncle John fail to notice he'd lost them? What happened when he finally discovered he was all alone? Did he stay at the market all day to sell his fruits and vegetables? Did he find Mother and Father by the side of the road on his way home? Were they OK? What happened when they all finally got back home?

When the story line was complete, the children acted it out: a stick for the horse, an invisible wagon behind it suggested by long string reins on both sides of the travelers, unpitched percussion accompaniment for the horse's sounds, and an Alto Xylophone ostinato for the wagon.

A short and simple folk tale can develop easily into a mini-opera at any level. With children in the lower grades, the teacher has the responsibility of keeping the accompanying patterns flowing, and should usually sing a recitative that keeps the story moving along. The children can do the unpitched percussion patterns and whatever simple chants and songs the class worked out. A few of them may be ready for simple solos, but avoid public performances at this level. Demonstrations are the thing, showing what's being accomplished without dinning it in or insisting on perfection. The point is to *play* with our materials.

I find I can use *From Wibbleton to Wobbleton* both as Speech Play and as an effective movement game.

*From Wibbleton to Wobbleton is sixteen miles;*
*From Wobbleton to Wibbleton is sixteen miles.*
*From Wibbleton to Wobbleton,*
*From Wobbleton to Wibbleton,*
*From Wibbleton to Wobbleton is sixteen miles!*

ENGLAND

For Speech Play, I like to use a relatively complicated patschen pattern with Wibbleton always on the right knee and Wobbleton on the left.

In the movement game, divide the class into Wibbletonian and Wobbletonian teams placed at opposite ends of the room. Students can move forward only when their town is mentioned in the rhyme and must freeze in place when the other team's moving.

Later, let them move on "sixteen miles" as well. This is great fun when young children are restless and need to move around for a while.

I also like to transfer this rhyme over to xylophones, with "Wibbleton" and "to" on low G and "Wobbleton" and "from" on low C. Play "sixteen miles" on alternating G's and C's or C's and G's.

Some of the insistently metrical rhymes, like "One, Two, Tie My Shoe," or "Hot Cross Buns," or "Jack, Jim Joe" are very useful when your classes are just learning their *Taa's, Ta-ti's* and *Taa-aa's,* and need to practice writing, saying, moving and playing them on sticks, wood-blocks, claves, or drums.

At this stage I like to give each child an envelope of rhythm cards in duple meter. These can be arranged to match names, words from different categories, and short rhymes. We combine name pairs to make longer patterns.

Later, a string of names that sound well together – of children, animals, food, reptiles, cars, or whatever else catches their fancy – and build more complicated patterns.

Then we move on to Question+Answer play. The sets of rhythm cards grow thicker as more duple patterns are introduced.

Soon we graduate to finding tunes to match the word rhythms or rhythm patterns we've chosen, or transfer them over to the timpani, unpitched percussion, or bar instruments.

Short rhymes provide a good foundation for class or solo improvisation and composition. Be sure to start with Speech Play and find many different ways to say each rhyme before settling on one, and before moving to any instruments or written notation.

Keep asking, "How else could you say it?" as you explore the possibilities. Keep patterns simple and complementary, whether for body percussion, unpitched percussion, or one or two bar instruments. Remember, the obvious is only the beginning.

Another favorite of primary children is my Rag Doll rhyme/story. I find that a lot of even young children are very tight and tense nowadays and need something like this to loosen up and learn to relax:

> *I'm just an old rag doll,*
> *I haven't any bones at all;*
> *I flip and I flop and I never quite know*
> *Just where my arms and legs will go!*
> *Kerflip, kerflop, kerflip, kerflop,*
> *I'm just an old rag doll, ...*
> *I haven't any bones at all. ....*
> *And suddenly ... down ... I ... fall.*

IMC

When everyone's lying on the floor I go around in and out among the children, lifting an arm or a leg and dropping it gently back onto the floor, when necessary reminding the tense ones that they haven't any bones.

Speech Play Exercises for Middle Grade Children (6-8)

With older children, separate teams can work out short scenes based on a familiar short folk tale or story. These scenes can include accompaniments, movement or appropriate dances, and some minimal costuming. Volunteers can work out a few recitatives, group songs, and solos to carry the story along. It seems to me far more valuable for the students to create their own mini-operas than to perform a run-of-the-mill, ready-made show in which there's no room for their own contributions and only the best singers and players have much to do.

My all-time favorite for this treatment is the Scottish version of Chicken Little I learned from a Scottish friend when I was a child. The speech itself is so musical that it needs no mini-arias or choruses – just sensitive musical speech with simple bordun/ostinato accompaniments by the teacher and capable students. Unfortunately it's too long to include here, but it's on the video of my Denver AOSA Conference session* if you want to learn it.

Song settings and body percussion are creative additions to songs and rhymes at any stage. Movement can accompany the speech play itself. Start by simply reinforcing the beat with clapping or a clap-patsch pattern. Later, divide the L-R patschen into two eighth notes, so the pattern becomes *taa (clap) ta-ti (L knee-R knee)*.

Keep a repertoire of simple body percussion patterns (from Schulwerk, Volume I, Part II) for use at a moment's notice. There are lots to choose from – and many more to invent.

---

* Available online to AOSA members in the video library https://aosa.org/resources/video-library/

Hand sign improvisation on two or three notes comes next, initially led by the teacher and later by student volunteers. When the children are ready, they learn to notate their tunes with stick notes and syllables, like this, for *Rain on the Green Grass:*

| So | So | So | La | La | So | So | So | Mi | |
|----|----|----|----|----|----|----|----|----|---|
| Rain | on | the | green | grass, | Rain | on | the | tree, | |

| So | So | So | La | Mi | Mi | So | So | La | |
|----|----|----|----|----|----|----|----|----|---|
| Rain | on | the | roof - | top, | but | not | on | ME! | |

A favorite of middle grade children is "I Saw Three Ships," with its invitation for individual choices of cargo. It requires accurate memory and lends itself to interesting body percussion accompaniment:

> *I saw three ships a-sailing on the Main,*
> *Three white ships a-sailing from Spain.*
> *Those three ships, a-sailing on the sea*
> *Were bringing* ten coconuts *home to me.*
> *What were they bringing to you?*

as the leader turns to his/her right-hand neighbor and the rhyme continues without breaking the rhythm. Each player in turn adds an additional item to the cargo as the game continues. Probably eight or ten players in each group will be enough. Each group chooses its own body percussion accompaniment.

Once the students know the game, it's fun to select a specific category for the cargo: animals, types of fruit, cars and trucks, etc.

Here's a useful chant game for canonic movement that I learned while teaching in Taiwan. The Chinese text couldn't be simpler, but the game's quite demanding and definitely for older students.

> *Saa sishi saa-aa,*
> *Saa sishi saa-aa,*
> *Saa sishi,*
> *Saa*
> *Saa sishi saa- aa.*

The class is divided according to experience and skill level into two, three, or four teams, with four or five students each.

Let me illustrate with two teams.

A student leader stands facing everyone, and while saying the chant, performs a simple, repetitive movement pattern. Both teams observe closely.

Then everyone on Team One says the chant and repeats the leader's movement. Just as they finish, the leader begins a second pattern.

Team One now imitates the second pattern, again saying the chant, while Team Two now does the *first* pattern and chants.

The leader goes on to a third pattern when Team One has finished; Team One imitates it while Team Two is doing the second pattern.

And so on, as each pattern is similarly passed along to the other team to perform.

It's quite a challenge, requiring very keen attention and memory, especially when there are more than two teams.

As to the patterns, choose ones like these, using (a) for older students and the stepping pattern (b) for adults:

*Pattern (a) Standing or Seated*

> *Stamp, clap, clap, patsch,*
> *Stamp, clap, clap, patsch,*
> *Stamp, clap, stamp, clap,*
> *Stamp, stamp, stamp.*

*Pattern (b) Stepping*

> *L together L (touch),*
> *R together R (touch),*
> *(forward) L together, (back) R together,*
> *L R, L R (in place).*

NOTE, in pattern (b) at "touch," you merely move one foot to touch your other foot, but don't shift your weight. So for example, Pattern (b) begins: step on Left foot, then step with Right foot to meet the Left, then step again on Left foot, then bring Right foot to meet it, but keep weight on the Left. This prepares for the following step on to the Right foot.

### Speech Play Exercises for Older Students and Adults

With older students and adults I like to begin Speech Play with a string of single words. For instance, I will write on the blackboard words suggested by the class for ways of walking: saunter, plod, amble, meander, stomp, limp, shuffle, tiptoe, zigzag, march. I ask a volunteer to get up and mime any one of the words for the class to guess. Then others in the class can join in and mimic the leader until another way of walking is chosen by the next volunteer.

Colors are great fun to play with too, since people have such strong feelings about them. I like to ask for suggestions from the class and invite five or six students whose choices flatter one another both rhythmically and otherwise to stand in front of the class; several feet apart. Initially I direct them, with whatever gestures each color suggests, repeating colors as often as I choose before moving on to another, in a very free rhythm, – not strictly metrical at all. At first, the colors may be in a set L – R sequence, along the line of volunteers; – later, in whatever sequence I choose. Volunteer directors can follow in my place, until we all tire of the color combinations and want to choose another set.

People love to play this game, whatever their age and stage. A couple of years ago, a group chose puce and chartreuse, which are NOT among my favorite colors. It was fun to inject a good deal of feeling into the color play as I lingered on those I liked and exaggerated my dislike of the others.

Older children and adults enjoy a more demanding name game with both a variety of accompanying body percussion patterns and amusing word play. It goes like this:

Jack, Mack,   rim‑ram rack,   Ree rye row and a   bob‑tailed back.

The players sit in a circle on the floor, and after the accompanying pattern's established, the leader starts of with the first verse and repeats it a time or two until it's secure. Then the fun begins, as each person in the circle says his/her name over the given pattern, inserting his/ her own name on the rhyming words like this:

*Isabel, Misabel, Rim, ram, Risabel, Ree rye row and a*
*bob-tailed Bisabel.*

Or:

> *Jerry, Merry, Rim, ram, Rerry, Ree rye, row and a*
> *bobtailed Berry.*

The next stage is based on folk sayings and short quotations. With a group of teachers, for example, I like to begin with one of Orff's most important sayings: "All song must come from speech." Then I ask: How would you say it? What's the obvious way? How else can you say it? Another way? Still another? What does he mean? I ask them to set it as a simple song, jotting down three or four possibilities in stick notes. Remember that *rests* are a great invention.

(For a list of more materials to play with, see Chapter 6, "Speech Play Resources.")

## Some Speech Play Exercises

Don't try to do everything at once!

While your class explores many types of exercises, it may take a number of weeks of delightful play to find out what a particular class most enjoys doing. And, of course, it can be quite different for each class, even though the developmental goal doesn't change. You want students to advance from simple Speech Play to accompanied song and movement. Let me suggest that if you are a teacher, you will want to build your own collection of rhymes and short poems that have some magic in them and which lend themselves to inventive, extended Speech Play.

Mid-grade or older children and adults enjoy this endlessly variable marching rhyme:

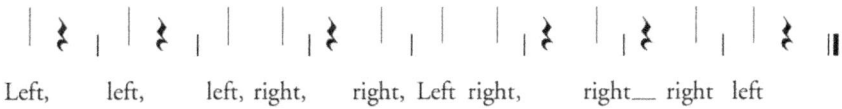

Left,      left,      left, right,      right, Left right,      right__ right left

I've also found it very useful with beginning recorder players, since any new note can be used with an already familiar one.

Vary the position of the rests as you play with this marching chant I heard soldiers singing as they marched up a hill in San Francisco years ago when I was attending the Bellflower Conference. They always used *Do* on the "lefts" and *So*, a fourth below, on the "rights."

Choose different leaders to lead the singing, each with his/her own variation for the class to join in on as they follow the leader around the room. Encourage the students to notate it simply with L, R and rests, like this:

$$2 \; \| \, \mathbf{L} \_\_ \quad \mathbf{L} \_\_ \quad \mathbf{L} \, \mathbf{R} \_\_ \, \mathbf{R} \, \| \; (etc.)$$

Here's another marching rhyme for your students to enjoy, with its delightful shift of accent in the third line. (It's also great fun to play on hand drums, once you work out the accentual shifts from right to left hand and back.)

> *Left __ , left __ , I had a good job and I left. __ ,*
> *Left my wife with twenty-four children without any*
> *    gingerbread.*
> *Did I do right, __ right, __ right by my country when I*
> *Left __ , left __ , I had a good job and I left ... etc.*

The Bangalory Man is a favorite for movement improvisation by the chosen "Bangalory Man," as several classmates form a line behind the student and imitate the student's movement. Follow the Bangalory man,

> *Follow the Bangalory man,*
> *I'll do all that ever I can,*
> *To follow the Bangalory man.*

The student leads the others around the room while the rest of the class chant and accompany the rhyme with body percussion and/or unpitched percussion.

There's lots of room for variations in tempo, movement, and style from one leader to another.

> *Infirtaris,*
> *Inoaknoneis*
> *In mudeelsare*
> *In claynoneis*
> *Goatseativy*
> *Mareseatoats.*

"Infirtaris" with its overlapping words has a mysterious air that makes it unusually stimulating for mock-serious unaccompanied speech play or a Klang Ostinato setting. Each line could be said by a different soloist, each of whom freezes in place until the rhyme is complete.

## Klang Ostinato (Soundscape) Settings

There are very few examples of sound settings of speech in the Schulwerk itself, and those that are included come almost as an afterthought, in Volume V in the section titled "Pieces using Speech", pages 1 1 1 ff., and in *Paralipomena*. There are, however, several examples appropriate for older students and adults included in my edition of *Carols and Anthems from the Schulwerk II*, including two speech choirs over three timpani in "Omnia Tempus Habent" and several examples of recitative and paraphony.

The term Klang Ostinato simply means "sound ostinato." There's no reason to postpone the technique until the advanced stages of Orff training. In fact, they work well from the very beginning, especially with short poems containing an element of magic.

Stories with repeated refrains provide a good beginning, as in my version of "Chicken Little" in which Chicken Little repeatedly says:

> *A black fairy flew*
> *Played nicky nicky noo*
> *On my silly poo.*
> *And I'm off to tell the King*
> *That Babbin's fallin'.*

For one Klang Ostinato setting, I added the bell tree after "flew," three taps on a wood-block on "nicky nicky noo," a triangle on "poo," and a hanging cymbal on "Babbin's" each time the rhyme recurred, with plenty of time between the lines.

There are many other short magical poems and a few folk rhymes that suggest the same free and minimal treatment, like Lillian Moore's "Until I Saw the Sea," or Lear's "Far and Few."

> *Far and few, Far and few*
> *Are the lands where the Jumblies live,*
> *Their heads are green*
> *And their hands are blue*
> *And they went to sea in a sieve.*

EDWARD LEAR (1812-1888)

Another is one of my favorite folk riddles from North Carolina, "Green as Grass."

> *Green as grass, and grass it's not;*
> *White as snow, and snow it's not;*
> *Red as blood, and blood it's not;*
> *Black as ink, and ink it's not.*
> *What is it? What is it?*
> *A blackberry! A blackberry!*

> NORTH CAROLINA

For older students, two favorites are "Night" by Sara Teasdale and the final verse of "Inversnaid" by Gerard Manly Hopkins.

> Night
> *Stars over snow,*
> *and in the West a planet*
> *Swinging below a star—*
> *Look for a lovely thing and you will find it;*
> *It is not far—*
> *It never will be far.*

> SARA TEASDALE (19TH C. AMERICAN
> POET)

> *From* Inversnaid (1881)
> *What would the world be, once bereft*
> *Of wet and of wildness? Let them be left,*
> *O let them be left, wildness and wet;*
> *Long live the weeds and the wilderness yet.*

> GERARD MANLY HOPKINS

Take time to say the texts aloud until everyone knows them by heart, trying different tempi, adding rests if needed, playing with the rhythm, the inflection, the timbre, the dynamics, until you find your own way of saying it together with that particular group.

Then consider the available sound possibilities that seem most appropriate for your chosen text. Keep the accompaniment thin, adding one instrument at a time to set the mood and scene, and the texture transparent, so the words come through. Sometimes only occasional punctuation is enough, with one or another percussion instrument at a time. Sometimes you may want to assign a solo voice to a line or two, or repeat a meaningful line *tutti*. Sometimes an ostinato or two seem appropriate.

Play with the possibilities. Each setting will be unique: the creation of that group, on that occasion.

Important!

Let me leave you with an urgent suggestion: Make your own collection of rhymes, poems, and stories. These should be particularly meaningful to you and worthwhile for your students to learn, play with, set to music, remember all their lives, and teach to their own children.

Nothing of lesser merit is worth either your time or theirs.

—

*While a portion of this essay appeared in The Orff Echo Volume 34 Issue 1 [Fall 2001], this extended version was previously unpublished. Portion reprinted with permission from The Orff Echo, the quarterly journal published by the American Orff-Schulwerk Association. This essay also draws on IMC's extensive notes, some of which appear to have been used for presentations she delivered on this topic. (See also the next chapter, "Speech Play Resources.")*

# 6  SPEECH PLAY RESOURCES

*Here is a collection of more of IMC's favorite rhymes, sayings, and suitable quotations for Speech Play. To the best of our knowledge, these are all in the public domain. Please enjoy!*

Ask yourself:

- Which of these rhymes suggest playing with inflection, tempo, and/or vocal color?
- Which suggest movement?
- Which require dramatic play?
- Which would work in canon?
- Which need a tune?
- Which need accompaniments?
- Which would work well in pairs?

Riddle Rhyme

### Riddle: As White As Milk

*As white as milk, as soft as silk,*
*And hundreds close together,*
*They sail away on a fine fall day*
*When windy is the weather.*

– CHEROKEE COUNTY, NC, ADAPTED
FROM WILHEMLINA SEEGMILLER (1866-
1913)

(Answer: Milkweed or dandelion after bloom.)

Counting Out Rhymes

*Too many horses in the stable,*
*Eeny, meeny, miney, mo,*
*One steps out.*
*This foot has got to go!*

*All the monkeys in the zoo,*
*Had their tails painted blue,*
*One , two, three,*
*Out goes you!*

*Little sinner, come to dinner,*
*Half past two.*
*Fried potatoes, alligators,*
*Out goes you!*

*One, two, sky blue,*
*One, two, three,*
*the bumblebee,*
*All out but you!*

*One, two, three, four, five,*
*I caught a fish alive,*
*Six, seven, eight, nine, ten,*
*I let him go again.*

*One, two, three, four,*
*Mary at the kitchen door,*
*Two, four, six, eight,*
*Mary at the garden gate.*

*One color, two color, three color, four,*
*Five color, six color, seven color, more!*
*What color is yours?*

*Eery, irie, ickery, ann*
*Fillasy, Pholasy, Nicholas, John*
*Queery Quavy Irish navy*
*Stringalum, stringalum, buck!*


*Seven blackbirds in a tree,*
*Count them and see what they may be:*
*One for sorrow,*
*Two for joy,*
*Three for a girl,*
*Four for a boy;*
*Five for silver,*
*Six for gold,*
*Seven for a secret that's never been told.*

ENGLAND


*Eenie meenie minie mo,*
*Catch a feeny finey foe*
*Omma nooja,*
*Oppa tooja,*
*Eenie meenie miney mo!*


*Eenie, meenie, hipperty dick*
*Oachie poachie dominochie*
*Ee, ta, too*
*Ugaly, bugaly, boo*
*Out goes you*

Traditional Rhymes

*Red sky at night,*
*Sailor's delight,*
*Red sky at morning,*
*Sailors take warning!*

*Jack Jim Joe*
*Bent his bow,*
*Shot at a pigeon*
*And killed a crow.*

BRITISH
COLUMBIA

*I have a dog and his name is Rover,*
*He is the one that I like best;*
*When he is good, he is good all over,*
*When he is bad, he is just a pest!*

USA

*Whistle and hoe,*
*Sing as you go,*
*Shorten the row*
*With the songs you know.*

USA

*It rained on Anne*
*It rained on Fran,*
*It rained on Arabella.*
*It did not rain*
*On Mary Jane;*
*She had a HUGE umbrella!*

ENGLAND

*Whether it's cold*
*Or whether it's hot,*
*There will be weather*
*Whether or not.*

ENGLAND

*Tinker tailor*
*Soldier sailor*
*Rich man, poor man,*
*Beggarman, thief*
*Doctor, lawyer,*
*Merchant, chief.*
*What about a pitcher,*
*Chemist, teacher?*
*What about a doctor,*
*Preacher, judge?*
*What about a biochemist,*
*Pilot, astronomer?*
*Singer, salesman,*
*Author, coach?*
*(add your own...)*

*Bonefish, bluebird, black sheep, crow*
*Chickadee, doodlebug, robins in a row*
*Banty rooster, peep squirrel, caterpillar, flea*
*Muley on the mountain and a big bumblebee*
*Fly in the cream jar, frog in the pool*
*Clap for all the children here at school*

PLAYGROUND RHYME,
CLEVELAND, OH

## Sayings

*Look before you leap.*

*Penny wise, pound foolish!*

*Time and tide wait for no man.*

*Take time while time is, for time will away!*

*Once is never enough.*

*Some are wise, and some are otherwise.*

*Work keeps at bay three great evils: boredom, vice, and need.*

VOLTAIRE

*He who MUST play cannot play.*

ADAM CARSE

*Don't look back! Someone may be gaining on you!*

SATCHEL PAIGE

*All song must come from speech.*

CARL ORFF

*A soft answer turneth away wrath.*

PROVERBS

*Silence is golden. Talk is cheap.*

*He who rises late must run all day.*


## Related Quotations

*A speech tone is never held as a sung note is held.*

CARL LEFEVRE


*The melodies of speech are a subtle and elusive music which require as much training as singing.*

SHALINI WADHWA


*Play is the basis of all art.*

CARL ORFF


*Movement is implicit in all music. Movement is doubly necessary: 1) as a means of externalizing and assimilating experience; as a form of expression; 2) as a gradual externalization of musical experience through motor activity, e.g. Hand signs.*

MICHAEL LANE


*Physical movement is the starting point for all musical knowledge.*

ANONYMOUS

More Rhymes

*Hinx, minx, the old witch winks*
*The fat begins to fry!*
*There's nobody home but Jumping Joan,*
*Father, Mother, and I!*


*Cataline and Cato,*
*Pericles and Plato,*
*All they would eat was*
*Cold boiled potato!*

ENGLAND


*Turvey, Turvey,*
*Clothed in black*
*With silver buttons all down your back;*
*One by one, and two by two,*
*Turn around, and that will do!*

ENGLAND


*Rings on her fingers and bells on her toes,*
*She shall have music wherever she goes.*

*Apples, peaches, pears, and plums,*
*Tell us when your birthday comes,*
*January (January), February (February),*
*March (March), April (April), etc.*

NOTE: *students call out in response when they hear the name of their birth month.*

*I won't be my father's Jack,*
*I won't be my father's Jill*
*I will be the fiddler's wife*
*And have music when I will*
*T'other little tune,*
*T'other little tune;*
*Prithee love, play me t'other little tune!*

*O Mother, I shall be married.*
*To Mr. Punchinello!*
*To Mr. Punch,*
*To Mr. Jo,*
*To Mr. Nell,*
*To Mr. Lo;*
*Mr. Punch,*
*Mr. Jo,*
*Mr. Nell,*
*Mr. Lo,*
*To Mr. Punchinello!*

Poems

### Moral

*For every evil under the sun*
*There is a cure or there is none.*
*If there be one, try and find it,*
*If there be none, never mind it.*

### Song from A Winter's Tale

*Jog on, jog on, the foot-path way,*
*And merrily hent the stile-a:*
*A merry heart goes all the day,*
*Your sad tires in a mile-a.*

SHAKESPEARE

*NOTE: "hent" means to take hold of; a "stile" provides steps over a fence that humans, not farm animals, can climb.*

*For, lo, the winter is past,*
*The rain is over and gone,*
*The flowers appear on the earth,*
*The time of the singing of birds is come,*
*And the voice of the turtle is heard in the land.*

FROM *THE SONG OF SOLOMON*

*This amusing old song was originally in a Dutch dialect. Keetman gave it a very perky setting and here's a rather free English translation. (IMC note.)*

1.

*There went a little priest down the lane,*
*It was in the May,*
*He took a little nun by the hand,*
*It was in the May, May, May,*
*It was in the May!*

2.

*O Little nun, will you walk with me?*
*The little priest took the nun along,*
*Over where the flowers be?*
*And they danced and danced to this silly song.*

Other examples (copyrighted materials)

*If I Could Go* – John Ciardi

*The Watch* – Walter de la Mare

*Two Cats* – Samuil Marshak

*Big Rocks into Pebbles* – Florence Parry Heide

*Trick or Treat* – Vachel Lindsay

See also Folk Rhymes and Sayings in Gertrud Orff's *Studies for Speech,* including: "He loves me, he don't"; "I see specks, specks see me"; "When the peacock loudly calls"; "Hitch your wagon to a star"; "A gift, a ghost, a friend, a foe"; "The sharper the blast"; "White bird featherless"; "Use every minute of today."

*This article was previously unpublished.*

# 7  AT THE FOOT OF THE MOUNTAINS
## (HOW MRS. DOW MADE A SONG)

*I discovered this original story with IMC's illustrations, dated 1989, among her manuscripts. If memory serves, it's loosely based on the actual experience of a woman my parents knew when they lived in New Mexico during the war. The story demonstrates the musicality of the spoken word and the progression from speech into song. Try reading it aloud!*

At the foot of the mountains, long ago and far away and before you were born or even dreamed of, I heard this story from my neighbor.

Who insisted it was really true.

At the foot of the desert mountains lived an old woman whose name was Mrs. Dow. She lived all by herself in her own adobe house with its faded blue doors and windows. There were two big cottonwood trees, one shading the front porch and the other near the old red barn in back, and along the road was a thick salt cedar hedge.

Old Mrs. Dow's hair was still black, and her skin was tan from the desert sun and wind, and she looked like the Pueblo people who lived in the mountains round about. She lived alone because she liked to live alone. And yet she was not alone at all. For on her ranch was a big billy goat whose name was William. A beautiful big collie dog whose name was Rex. A flighty black cat called Clinker. A pet rooster named Harold, who thought he was king of the barnyard. And a large white goose called Clemmie, who was named after Mrs. Dow's first cousin Clementine.

One bright blue day, Mrs. Dow looked in the pantry and found she was out of eggs and sugar. There was no mash for William, no bone for Rex, no fish for Clinker, and only a few grains of corn were left for Harold and Clemmie. So she hung up her yellow apron behind the kitchen door and off she went to the old red barn where she kept her Model T car. She got in and slammed the door, then she backed out in a cloud of reddish dust and turned onto the road that led into town.

As she drove slowly along, she was saying over to herself so she wouldn't forget: Sugar and eggs for me alone; mash for William; for Rex a bone; fish for Clinker; five pounds of corn.

*Rex the dog (by IMC)*

Pretty soon it started turning into a song. And she began to enjoy singing it, softly at first, then louder and louder, feeling very pleased with herself:

> *Sugar and eggs for me alone,*
> *Mash for William, for Rex a bone,*
> *Fish for Clinker, five pounds of corn.*

She kept singing and humming and singing and changing it until it was just right:

> *Sugar and eggs for me alone,*
> *Mash for William, for Rex a bone,*
> *Fish for Clinker, Five pounds of corn*
> *For Harold and Clemmie to eat each morn.*

Approaching the Hanes' house, she saw young Mike out in the front yard. He was swinging lazily on an old tire hanging from a big cottonwood. But as she came closer, he jumped off and ran back to the house. He was laughing and shouting: "Mom, Dad, Sarah! Come quick!" And they all came scrambling out the kitchen door, bursting out laughing just as much as Mike himself as soon as they saw the car.

"Funny," Mrs. Dow thought. "What could they be carrying on about?"

She went back to singing her song, changing the tune a little till she liked it even better. She had just got to "for Rex a bone" for the third time when Billy Shaw came bicycling toward her, whistling happily, with a sack of groceries in his basket. She smiled and waved at him. Then just as he came even with the car, he shouted out "Holy cow!" and burst out laughing so hard that his bicycle started making snake tracks all over the dusty road.

What had come over her neighbors? What was so funny? What could possibly be so funny?

Had she forgotten to take off her yellow apron? No. She glanced down and saw her new blouse was still fresh and neat. How about her hair? That's when she looked in the car mirror. And what do you think she saw?

There behind her was William, goat trotting along seriously.

And behind William was Rex, alert as a guard dog, wagging his tail.

And behind Rex was Clinker, darting catlike ahead then hanging back.

And behind Clinker was Harold, scurrying and fanning his rooster wings.

And last of all Clemmie, stretching her long goose neck, squawking and flapping, trying to keep up!

At that very moment, Mrs. Dow arrived at the schoolhouse on the edge of town. She checked the mirror again, and blinked to make sure she wasn't seeing things. The animals looked so tired.

What would you have done? She knew what to do.

All the schoolchildren were outside for recess, and they froze in amazement in the middle of their games. They watched as Mrs. Dow turned the car completely around and started back the way she had come. William and Rex and Clinker and Harold and Clemmie fell solemnly in line behind, and they all headed slowly for home.

As she drove back past the Hanes' house, Mrs. Dow saw the whole family at the parlor window, grinning from ear to ear. When she reached the Shaws' place, they were outside the kitchen door, laughing till tears ran down their faces. And Big Joe Brown, out in his melon patch, stopped hoeing and roared as she went past. No one had seen such a parade before, not even at the circus.

When the car reached home at last, William and Rex and Clinker and Harold and Clemmie all collapsed in the shade of the big cottonwood near the old barn. Mrs. Dow put the car back in the old barn and hurried into her cool kitchen. She called Smithers Grocery in town and she ordered: one dozen eggs, a pound of sugar, ten pounds of mash, two soup bones, three cans of fish, and five pounds of corn.

Clemmie the Goose (by IMC)

It wasn't long before Jim, the grocer's boy, rattled into the barnyard in his noisy old truck. Out he got, with the curious animals crowding around him as he carried a big cardboard box into the kitchen, settling it on the counter with a cheerful greeting. Mrs. Dow paid him. A moment later he was on his way, rattling back to town.

As she unpacked the box, she sang her song again and again, until everything was put away where it belonged.

> *Sugar and eggs for me alone,*
> *Mash for William, for Rex a bone,*
> *Fish for Clinker, Five pounds of corn*
> *For Harold and Clemmie to eat each morn.*

While all the animals rested in the shade and the shadows grew longer and longer and bluer and bluer, the old woman fixed a picnic in her yellow kitchen. Soon across the valley the mountains began turning from deep blue to purple and a gentle breeze came rustling through the cottonwoods.

When she came out the kitchen door with a loaded tray, all the animals followed her over to the big cottonwood by the old red barn.

She put the tray on a table. Then she set down a bowl of mash in front of William. She laid the biggest bone in front of Rex. She put Clinker's blue bowl full of fish in her favorite place. And she tossed two handfuls of corn on the ground for Harold and Clemmie. Then she picked up her own plate and sat down at the table.

In the cool of the evening, she nibbled her devilled eggs and potato salad, enjoying each bite, and sipped her hot sugared coffee. William the goat gobbled his mash as if he'd never eaten in his whole life before. Rex the dog chomped on his bone, breaking it with his sturdy teeth to get at the marrow. Clinker the cat daintily curled her tongue around every morsel of her fish. Harold the rooster and Clemmie the goose greedily pecked at their corn, tipping their heads back to swallow while keeping an eye on each other to make sure neither got more than a fair share.

When all had finished their picnic meals, they sat contentedly while the twilight deepened to darkness and the stars came out one by one. It was very quiet. Sometimes a breeze rustled in the cottonwoods. Sometimes a lone car buzzed along the road.

*Harold the Rooster (by IMC)*

Before long, the animals headed off to bed. William went to his pen. Rex curled up at the back door. Clinker sat in her favorite chair on the front porch. Harold and Clemmie nestled down in the barnyard.

The old woman picked up the dirty dishes, put them on the tray, and made her way to the kitchen in the dark. When she'd done the dishes, off she went to bed, too, humming her new song to herself:

*Sugar and eggs for me alone,*
*Mash for William, for Rex a bone,*
*Fish for Clinker, Five pounds of corn*
*For Harold and Clemmie to eat each morn.*

Sleepily, she smiled, remembering the day's surprising little parade.

—

*This story was previously unpublished.*

# 8  INTRODUCING OSTINATI WITH MURRAY VOLUME I

*For the teacher, preparing a new class to create the Carpet of Sound – the sonic trademark of the Orff Approach – can be daunting. This essay reviews the steps, with references to Murray Volume I as source material for exercises and inspiration. Also, there's a handy series of questions for analyzing any new piece under consideration for use in the Orff classroom.*

## Before the Bar Instruments

As anyone trained in Orff knows, the easily recognized bar instruments are often what people associate most with the Orff Approach. Yet, we also know that the best way to introduce students to using the instruments is with preliminary work. Along with speech, and movement, I introduce ostinati using body percussion and unpitched percussion. In the Orff-Schulwerk Volumes, suggestions for body percussion patterns begin on page 60 of Volume I of the Murray edition.

A quick glance shows a surprisingly rapid progression, with only a single line of clapping patterns, ten examples of stamp-clap patterns, and two lines each of three- and four-movement patterns, with not a single patschen exercise until page 76. Again, we need to sequence these examples, and insert many easy variants of the easiest patterns for use in our own classrooms.

The first rhythm pieces over ostinato accompaniments follow on pages 62 and 63, starting with stamp-clap patterns that would be impossible for Kindergarteners and primaries to do. It would be wiser to use a simple patschen exercise reinforcing the beat or a patsch-clap ostinato, which is more likely to keep steady because of its required up and down movement. With little people, I'd substitute the rhythm of a folk rhyme they'd already explored in speech play for the rhythm solo rather than attempt to teach an abstract rhythm piece like this.

With older children, such as Orff and Keetman were working with, these pieces could be done as written or with small changes in the ostinato parts to match the skill of the class. (Remember that the feet are intended to alternate on the stamps, although the notation doesn't make this clear.)

## Unpitched Percussion

These pieces also transfer very effectively to unpitched percussion instruments. There are some wonderful rhythmic rondos in this section which older classes would thoroughly enjoy doing as written. Later, revisit them, adding movement, and substituting rhythm instruments for body percussion. When only the Rondo theme is given, students would enjoy developing their own contrasting episodes to complete their own rondos.

Many of the pieces in this section and in Volume V Part II transfer very effectively to hand drums and other percussion instruments. They're particularly good for small group assignments to be worked out with movement, or extended with solo or group improvisation. All of them provide a stimulating basis for movement improvisation and composition.

## The Orff Ensemble

The instrumental pieces in Part III begin on page 94 of Volume I in the Murray edition with two relatively simple pieces. Older children could learn them quite easily, but for little people we would need to simplify them and probably reassign them from glockenspiels to xylophones and metallophones, with their larger bars. In #1, the metallophone could play the Alto Glockenspiel part as written in the A section, with a dotted half and a quarter in bars two and four of the B section to keep the movement going. The melody on Soprano Xylophone and Alto Xylophone in the higher octave would take a good deal of time for the children to work out because the sticking is not obvious. Even with older children, a steady beat on Bass Xylophone or a quiet C timp would help keep the piece together, since it takes a very secure child to play whole notes without rushing.

Number 2 on page 94 would be much easier with a steady beat in the lower part, though the interruption of the accompaniment in the B section might prove a problem. I'd prefer to keep the rising pattern going, to G and D' for three beats and to C' and E' at the end.

Most Orff teachers have likely taught the piece on page 95 again and again, or at least learned it in Level I. It is very skillfully arranged, with a simple introduction for all the accompanying instruments on G and a triangle on the rests, and continuous parts throughout the piece itself. Probably you could do it with middle graders successfully without having to change it at all. There are parts for children at different levels of skill. Which are the easiest? The most difficult? If necessary, you could divide the AX part between two players. You might choose to reassign the melody to recorders, or play it yourself until the tune's familiar to the children, at least while the class is working on the ostinati. Once the tune's in their ears, it will be much easier for them to learn, since the sticking will be the only problem.

It is interesting to look at the other version of this piece on page 98. How much is the same? Is it easier or more demanding? What would be the teaching problems? If the children were sure of the form, from your playing the melody first (A A B A), the only real problem would be the two bars of the B section, simply because they're different. If you assign them to three soloists, the piece will jell in no time. Then the major problem will be the dynamic contrast between the *piano* introduction and B section and the *forte* A sections.

I particularly enjoy the little pieces on pages 104 to 106 which are scored for only three parts, with the melody unassigned. They are short enough that they can be worked out quickly, in small group assignments to be brought back to the whole class, used to accompany movement in pairs, small groups, or all who are not playing. Or they can be developed with new improvised sections over the same ostinati, or with patterns from other pieces.

These short pieces provide a fine opportunity for the more capable students when the rest of the class needs more practice on something they've already mastered. And I like the opportunity to choose the timbre for the melody. Voices and recorders – which appear only twice in Volume I in difficult scores, which Keetman must have played herself – provide alternatives to the glockenspiels and xylophones – the only bar instruments available when these pieces were written. The solo assignment will, of course, depend on the ranges of the chosen accompanying instruments, since the octave relationships need to be maintained.

The students will also learn a good deal about arranging pieces for the ensemble by working out these pieces to suit themselves. When you want to use your whole ensemble at once for more than multiple ostinato practice, consider the possibility of assigning one part to the highs, the other to the lows, or one to the metals and the other to the woods. That way, everyone has a chance to learn the new patterns and techniques introduced in these pieces and the others in this section of Volume I.

### Questions for Analysis

Let's look at #20 on page 106 and ask a series of questions always valuable when analyzing a piece for possible use:

- *What is the scale?* Do Pentatonic in the C setup.
- *The range of the melody?* C to A.
- *The form?* Introduction / A (a a') / B (b b') / A.
- *The mood?* Relaxed and quietly lyrical, as if singing to oneself.
- *Are the ostinati continuous throughout?* Yes.
- *Are there any new techniques?* Yes: Irregular sticking in the Alto Glockenspiel part, with four eighths in the Right hand and two in the Left. It also requires three-mallet technique in the Alto Xylophone part, which looks much more alarming than it is, since the Right hand stays on the same two notes throughout while the Left moves stepwise, G-G-A-A, in every bar.
- *How could you simplify the ostinati?* By dividing the parts, and playing steady eighths instead of the more demanding printed pattern. But if there's a child who can do each as written, by all means let him or her do so.
- *Do you see any problems in teaching this piece?* Both ostinato parts would require body percussion preparation, simply moving the hands on a desktop to fit the AG pattern, and practicing the AX pattern alternating hands on knees to accompany the melody before attempting it on the xylophone.
- *How would you introduce the melody?* Probably with hand-sign singing, since it's in an easy range. Challenge the

students to figure out the form for themselves as you play it for them, so they hear the change in the repeat of *a* and the exact repetitions of *b*. Once they know the tune, ask for suggestions for reassigning the melody to different instruments, and let the students try them out then and there, discussing each change in turn and choosing the best solutions to use in class, either in succession, or with transitions between them.

- *How could you make use of it, once the students know it well?* Perhaps for a small group to play for mirror movement by the rest of the class. Or for a lullaby in a fairy tale. Or as a transition between large numbers for a small group to play in a demonstration while the others are changing places, getting ready for the next piece. Or for small groups to work out together, with soloists playing while the others devise their own simple partner or circle dance, and with all the groups sharing their solutions afterwards.

## Gradual Complexity

With preschoolers and primaries it is wise to use only one bar instrument ostinato at a time (which may, of course, be doubled) until they've had a lot of experience accompanying rhymes, short poems and simple songs with basic bilateral or alternating patschen patterns, or simple combinations of slap-clap movements. Steady eighths need practice too, most easily with patschen, hands together.

Patterns combining quarters and eighths in a simple pattern like *Taa, taa, ta-ti, taa*; *Taa ta-ti, taa ta-ti*; or *Taa taa ta-ti ta-ti* come next, as soon as the students are ready. At the same time, even young children are quite capable of improvising and experimenting on the bar instruments, working out their own tunes on two or three notes for rhymes they already know. They can also learn simple songs from books designed for young beginners.

Remember: There's no hurry. Children have all the time in the world.

The longer pieces in Part III of the instrumental section are very challenging and rewarding for older children. Probably the best known are the Rondo on page 111, which most Orff teachers have probably done in Level I, the very rhythmical Dance Rondo starting on page 123, and the following Rondo, pages 128-30.

There are many other pieces worth studying and performing. Many of them are far more demanding than most of the material in Volume II, and would make a valuable addition to the repertoire for higher grades.

Pentatonic is not synonymous with easy, and we need never leave it behind, particularly when Volume I has introduced only *Do* Pentatonic, and only in the authentic position (*Do* to *Do'*). Most of our folk songs, in contrast, are plagal (*So* to *So'*), and our children need practice in at least the F and G setups on the bar instruments.

They also need experience with the other pentatonic modes, which are still alive in our own folk traditions, though they are largely ignored in conventional music education.*

When you're looking for pentatonic songs to arrange for your own classes, the best sources are Louise Bradford's *Sing It Yourself*, Alfred, a rich collection of 220 American pentatonic folk songs sequenced according to their vocal ranges. Bradford's book includes three and four-note tunes at the beginning to those requiring a range of a tenth or eleventh at the end, complete with notes and sources, a useful list of the songs, and instructions for all the singing games. I also recommend my books, *My Recorder Reader* 1 and 2 from Brasstown Press, which contain songs in a variety of pentatonic modes sequenced according to their ranges.

---

* See "The Pentatonic Scales and Modes," p 247.

Many of these songs are in plagal position, a welcome relief from an overdose of *Do* Pentatonic in Volume I, and an essential step in developing skill at the bar instruments, since all the patterns have to be either transposed or altered to fit the unfamiliar range with *Do* in the middle of the melody, not at either end.

The range from *So* to *So'* encourages the development of more interesting melodic improvisation, since the tune naturally circles around the final instead of moving either up or down.

This is also true of the melodies in *Re*, *So*, and *La* Pentatonic modes, which not only wean the students away from *Do* in preparation for the diatonic modes later on, but change the position of the tunes and patterns on the instruments.

*Re* Pentatonic, for instance, permits a characteristic modal cadence from the low seventh, C in the C Pentatonic setup, to the final on D, and provides a complete major chord on the seventh degree.

The different placement of the gaps in the scale in the various pentatonic modes completely changes the character of the melodies, and provides new tonal realms to explore. There's no need to rush into the more familiar hexatonic and diatonic tunes of our heritage.

—

*While portions of this essay first appeared in The Orff Echo Volume 27 Issue 1 [Fall 1994], this extended version was previously unpublished. The Orff Echo is the quarterly journal published by the American Orff-Schulwerk Association.*

# PART 3

## EDUCATING THE EDUCATORS

**E**

*Mi*

# EDUCATING THE EDUCATORS

*The teacher needs to be a model for student playing,
so that they hear what to aim for.*

ISABEL MCNEILL CARLEY

# 9  TIPS FOR TEACHERS OF THE RECORDER

*Here, IMC consolidates and organizes her vast experience teaching recorder. Of interest to Orff teachers of all persuasions, this essay in outline form provides all the steps needed to build a successful recorder track in an Orff curriculum.*

Many of these teaching tips are particularly applicable for classes of children, but may be equally useful at any age or stage of instruction – although the application may require modifications. The classification scheme is necessarily somewhat arbitrary, but for our purposes they are arranged in five useful categories: I. Tips for Children; II. Tips for All Beginners; III. Tips for All Students; IV. Reminders for Improvisation Lessons; and V. A Few Basic Principles.

Applying these teaching tips rigorously for students of any age will result in better recorder technique and much faster progress than using any other approach I have ever tried.

Introducing the Recorder

Recorder beginners of any age will learn and progress much faster when they have a good idea of what tone to strive for and how breath control and articulation can produce it. This should happen before they get preoccupied with notation. Tone-matching exercises and echo-play easily point beginners in the right direction. First, play on one note. Then on two. With older children and adults, I like to begin with C' and A, the falling third, which is the natural chant of childhood and the basic interval for both the Orff Approach and the Kodály Method. For younger children, I use the same interval, transposed to G down to E, thus involving both young hands right away.

Why begin with imitation? For two reasons: aural memory and inner hearing. These must be developed before individual musical ideas can be expressed. Of course, one has to have some tonal vocabulary to work with. The teaching of each new recorder note and its combinations is simply best accomplished through imitative exercises.

I. Tips For Children

1. To develop proper breath support, ask the children in their chairs to reach down and pick up two "invisible" suitcases, one on a side. They will automatically begin to exhale as they reach down and then support their breath with an impulse from the solar plexus as they "lift" the suitcases. When they're sitting tall, let them silently "drop" their suitcases back down.

While the soprano recorder requires little breath, it does require control, which is possible only with proper support and posture. When the suitcase trick palls, ask the children to pick up an imaginary baseball and prepare to throw it on signal. (Use a triangle as a signal, or whatever you choose.) Repeat without completing the throwing motion, but have them put the imaginary ball down while maintaining the feeling of vitality in their bodies.

2. For each child, provide anchors or thumb rests for the right thumb. This way the thumb can't wander wildly around the instrument before the right hand gets more into the act.

3. Use Building Block rhythmic patterns as a basis for melodic improvisation. (Duplicate cards will be required; still more cards later on.) In 2/4 meter, these would be your patterns

Make up a four-card rhythm phrase using any of these cards. This will make the most sense, especially for rank beginners, if at least one of the cards is used twice or even three times. For example:

  a. When the class knows only one note, probably B, ask
     them to:

- clap and say the rhythm, using French time names.
- finger and tongue in rhythm ("Dah, dah," etc.)
- play what they see, on B.

  b. When they know two notes, ask them to:

- clap and say the rhythm, as before.
- finger silently, alternating notes throughout, B A B A B, etc. or A B A B etc.
- play, listening for both neighbors.

  c. When they have advanced to three or more notes, ask
     them to:

- clap and say the rhythm as before.
- finger silently the notes you indicate with Hand Signs.
- play while you lead with the same Hand Sign tune.

Keep the game going as long as you choose by changing the four-card pattern each time, or by allowing the first volunteer to play it solo for the class to echo. If correct, the volunteer may change one card in the pattern by removing it and either replacing it with a new card or with another card in the current pattern.

## II. Tips for All Beginners

1. Music is an aural art. It must be approached through the ear, not the eye. Hence the need for echo-play and improvisation – not only for beginners, but also for all aspiring players. The teacher needs to be a model for student playing so that they hear what to aim for – in tone, style, tempo, articulation, dynamics, etc. They need a clear Gestalt of the mood and aura of any piece before they start to practice it on their own.

Psychologists tell us that, when learning something new, both sides of our brain will cooperate far better if an idea of the *whole* (song, poem, article, book) is given beforehand. This prevents the learner from hopelessly bogging down in any one particular section that logical written sequencing dictated.

2. To achieve Good Articulation and Tone from the very beginning, make echo-play warm-ups part of every lesson, and insist on meticulously accurate echoes with the exact tonguing and articulation of the initial phrase. Make a point of using all possibilities in different phrases.

- Tongued legato: d-th, d-g, d-t – or whatever works best for you.

- Portato: dah(t) dah(t) – leaning into the notes and separating them slightly, like a cello playing separate bowings.
- Staccato: d(t) d(t) – as short as the tempo requires
- Slurs – so there are no unintentional wisps of sound between the notes.
- Rests – silences of articulation where punctuation is required.
- Phrase-breaks, releases, and phrase-endings.

3. Since rhythm is basic to all music making, rhythmic training must be basic to music teaching. This means *movement*, not counting, since the rhythm must be in the muscles, not in the left brain. Music is not arithmetic.

4. Rhythmic problems always have rhythmic solutions (which involve multisensory exercises including movement). Students can:

- Clap and say the troubling pattern, with time names or nonsense syllables.
- Step the beat in place and CLAP the troublesome pattern over and over.
- Play the pattern on a rhythm instrument while walking to the teacher's drum.
- Use the pattern as an ostinato on a rhythm or bar instrument to accompany solo improvisation.

Ask everyone to work out their own Dance Step that exactly matches the rhythm pattern, and work out several class dances using these improvised steps in small groups. Use rhythm instrument accompaniment, if you choose.

5. Teach only one thing at a time. When more than one element is involved, be doubly sure that the older element is secure enough to be "automatic" before anything new is demanded.

- Rhythm Clapping comes first with beginners. Then, do fingering and tonguing aloud in rhythm, with recorders on chins.
- Fingering notes while saying note names.
- Playing slowly and steadily over the teacher's steady drumbeat, which sets the tempo before everyone enters.
- Practicing, over and over, until tempo and articulation are correct.
- Playing up to tempo.

6. Sight-Reading Skills are developed through the use of much material simple and familiar enough in style and technical demands that almost immediate success is virtually guaranteed. The teacher's job is to find the repertoire that is both musically rewarding and technically simple enough for the class to enjoy.

7. Releases require as much attention as attacks. Have students tuck their tongues up behind the upper teeth to prevent any air escaping, like a silent T. Then you will not have to endure the ugly wisps of sound that dangle from a cadence or final chord when students are inattentive.

8. *Festina lente* (Latin, meaning "make haste slowly") so TAKE YOUR TIME. There is no hurry to learn new notes. Far better to have your students play simple things with style, good tone, and musical understanding than to move so fast that their muscles are tied up in knots with anxiety and they can't concentrate on the sound they're producing.

9. Muscles are slow learners. Hence the need for practice, much repetition, and a slow pace, using a wide range of repertoire at each level of achievement. Many beginners internally hear what they want to produce but are unable to play what they hear. They become depressed with their slow progress, and need constant reassurances that muscles learn much mores slowly than minds.

After the first enthusiasm, there is always a slump when students begin to realize that making music requires far more effort than the apparent ease of the professionals they see playing on TV had led them to expect. They need to be told of the years of training and practice that all teachers and professional performers have undergone to reach their present level.

10. To develop reading skills, practice with simple repertoires requiring sight-reading, both in class lesson time and private practice. The teacher's job is to find a repertoire that is musically rewarding and at the same time technically simple enough that success for the student is almost guaranteed.

11. When students can really play a piece, it's time to play with the piece as well. Make up variations through a change of mode, meter, tempo, articulation, dynamics, range, timbre, or form. Transform a simple andante Song into a proud Pavane, an elegant Waltz, a perky Scherzo, a somber Funeral March, a vigorous Polka, or a sleepy Lullaby. Or whatever else you or your students may imagine. At a later stage, you can introduce melodic ornamentation in Renaissance style.

## III. Tips for All Students

1. "A musical score is like a map," said composer Ralph Vaughan Williams. "It bears no more relation to the art of music than does a road map to the outside world." Good playing – musical playing – depends on the students' ability to hear both what they are doing and what's going on around them.

2. There is nothing more important than choosing music worth a thorough study by the teacher and serious practice by the student. Take the time to study the catalogs of current offerings from major dealers and publishers. Once selected music is in your hands, spend the necessary time to analyze it thoroughly.

- What is the piece's form?
- What are the problems in fingering, in technique, in interpretation, in ensemble playing?
- How will you use it? In performance? As a basis for dramatic play? For dance movement? As an example of a historical style?

THEN teach it.

3. Work on your own recorder skills, as you will be the model for your students' playing. Your own tone, articulation, and style will determine what you hear from your students. Play new pieces through for them to demonstrate what you want, instead of talking. Then they will grasp a clear Gestalt of the mood and aura of the piece before they start their own practice. Without this, you will need to spend your time correcting mistakes rather than making music – and we're told that making corrections takes ten times as long as learning correctly in the first place.

4. The teacher's skilled use of a hand drum or a bar instrument to maintain a steady pulse, or an ostinato, during echo-play and other warm-up activities relaxes the natural group tension. This supports short assignments while students briefly wait for their turns. The continuous rhythm minimizes the awkward breaks when someone falls short, and keeps the activity moving in spite of occasional goofs. The rhythm itself will provide a security blanket with an almost hypnotic continuity that conceals errors and supports risk-taking.

5. Notes are never enough. Music lives only when it comas alive in the minds of students. This is possible only when the music is tailored to technical and musical development, and when it has been memorized or so well practiced that student interpretation becomes possible.

Aural sensitivity and discrimination can best be cultivated through improvisation and memorization, that is, when there are no visual distractions to engage the left brain's attention. Therefore it is important to include at least a minimum of improvisation in every lesson, and to take the time to play and polish the pieces the students already know thoroughly. It is only then that interpretation becomes possible.

6. Punctuation is as important to music as it is in language. Silences of articulation, rests, clear phrase breaks, artfully performed slurs (with the weight on the first note and the second slightly shortened and light) are all-important for stylistic clarity. It's particularly true in the Baroque style, where each little motif must stand alone, set off by silences of articulation from its neighbors.

7. The pentatonic scales of G, C, and F match up well with the technique of the recorder, avoiding awkward cross-fingerings and shifts until all the notes of the diatonic scale are learned. Then it becomes simply a matter of putting together what one already knows – what one's fingers are used to doing – and moving from E to F and from B to C to D' to play the full scale of C and all its related modes.

With the addition of Bb and F#, the realms of the G scale and the F scale are completed, with all their attendant modal riches. The remaining chromatic fingerings –C#, D#, and G# – may be introduced one by one as needed. Certainly there's no hurry, not if we choose to follow the Orff progression in our recorder teaching, as I prefer to do. So, I like to begin with G Pentatonic. It lies in the plagal position on the soprano recorder (*Do* in the middle of the range). By far the majority of American folk songs are in this plagal position.

Then C Pentatonic: CDE GA C'D'E' (G'A'). Then G hexatonic with C, which is already familiar; fine muscle control must be developed enough to manage the B C' D' C' switches. Then F Pentatonic (FGA C'D' F'G'A') to secure both F's.Then C hexatonic with F. And finally, the missing cross-fingerings to complete the diatonic scales of G (F#) and F (Bb) to enable exploration of the related modal scales before any new fingering is introduced. But then, only one at a time, as the repertoire requires.

8. Each new diatonic scale can best be practiced through SCALE-TUNE ECHO-PLAY. The rules are:

- The improvised scale phrase must use all the notes of the scale, ascending or descending.
- Notes may be repeated as much as needed en route to make a convincing tune.
- No backtracking is allowed.
- The tune must be a phrase, a musical idea, with clear meter, rhythm, articulation, and a characteristic rhythmic or melodic motif, if possible

9. Harmonic progressions, in closed or open positions, can be worked out spontaneously once the students know the basic traditional functional progressions:

$$I - V - I; I - IV - I ; I - IV - V - I .$$

Each part is assigned one note of the chord and moves to the closest note of the next chord on signal. The teacher holds up one, four, or five fingers, repeating or shifting chords at will, and indicates the rhythm with gestures.

Charts of typical progressions may be used later (derived from repertoire the students are playing) or designed for later development. For example:

*Closed Position*

| Soprano Recorder | | D' | E' | D' | | D' | D' | D' | | D' | E' | D' | D' |
|---|---|---|---|---|---|---|---|---|---|---|---|---|---|
| Alto | | B | C | B | | B | A | B | | B | C | A | B |
| Tenor | | G | G | G | | G | F# | G | | G | G | F# | G |
| Triads: | | I | IV | I | | I | V | I | | I | IV | V | I |

*Open Position*

| Soprano | | B | C | B | | B | A | B | | B | C | A | B |
|---|---|---|---|---|---|---|---|---|---|---|---|---|---|
| Alto | | D | E | D | | D | D | D | | D | E | D | D |
| Tenor | | G | G | G | | G | F# | G | | G | G | F# | G |
| Triads: | | I | IV | I | | I | V | I | | I | IV | V | I |

Inversions would be approached in the same way.

Such exercises provide ideal warm-ups for consort playing, particularly in tandem with scale-tune improvisation using the key of the next piece to be played. Intonation will be far more accurate from the beginning when the group is already "tuned in" to the tonality. Such chordal exercises will need to be expanded to match the repertoire, particularly for the Renaissance and Early Baroque modal repertoire that was composed before such obvious functional harmony developed.

10. Repetition and contrast are the basis of musical form, whether in repertoire or improvisation. A new piece becomes far less daunting when students have heard it before playing it themselves, or have already looked at the score to analyze the basic form. Then they will recognize the piece's repetitions as familiar territory before they plunge in, and can prepare to spend more time practicing the less-frequently occurring contrasting sections.

## IV. Reminders for Improvisation Lessons

1. Rhythmically secure ostinato/drone accompaniments encourage free melodic improvisation at a level impossible to reach without that reassuring and supporting Carpet of Sound. Such continuous patterns – or combination of overlapping patterns in complementary ranges and colors – engage and release the right brain as "bare" improvisation seldom does. This allows our natural musicality to come out of hiding and, particularly in public, to play like a composer with the materials of music.

2. Hand Signs insure better pitch in the early stages of playing recorder, and permit free and instantaneous group improvisation. EVERYONE in the classroom can follow the teacher (or volunteer leaders) in Question+Answer play, one phrase at a time until it's perfect.

The use of Hand Signs is not a childish technique to be cast aside as soon as students can read notation. Valuable as it is in the initial stage of translating visual signs to sounds, it continues to be a very helpful technique for drilling rough spots or introducing new melodies. Hand Sign tunes provide a visual image in place of the usual aural cues for echo-play, but depend on aural memory as well as visual decoding. At the same time, this fits the natural learning style of the visual learners in the class while developing visual decoding skills in the kinesthetic and aural learners.

And the technique works at any stage.

The next variation is QUESTION+ANSWER PLAY. A leader signs the QUESTION and another signs the ANSWER while the entire rest of the group is playing at sight. Volunteers only at first, please. Later, you can allow free melodic improvisation.

3. The best opportunity to discover the individual musical level of each student is in improvisation lessons. This is demanding on the teacher's ability to tailor particular assignments to the ability of the individuals in the group. But successfully done, a growing musical sensitivity is guaranteed.

4. Chord progressions such as those at Item 9 above, provide an ideal foundation for solo melodic improvisation. When the time comes, the soloist can play on sopranino over SAT, keeping the accompanying Soprano in its low range so as not to interfere with the solo line.

I have always found it helpful to have the students SING these chord changes and improvise vocally before transferring over to recorders. Such exploration leads naturally into Orff's "thirding around," also known as "Umterzen," or "decorating the third," as Margaret Murray puts it. (See Murray Volume IV, page 118ff, and again in Murray V, page 33.) Then you can move on to Renaissance-style "divisions" and heterophony, the simultaneous ornamentation of the basic melody, usually in a higher range.

5. Quotable IMC Tips on Improvisation.

- Repeated notes are a great invention.
- Some of the greatest melodies are stepwise.
- Leaps are usually reserved for emphasis.
- The simpler the melody and the more restricted the range, the more it needs short rhythmic motives to bring it to life.
- No one ever improvised beyond his or her own ability.
- Listen to where the melody wants to go – as Orff used to say. Trust your own musical instincts.
- Keep going once you start. It may be better than you think.
- Make use of your mistakes. No one else knows what you intended unless you tell them.

6. Allow yourself and your students to PLAY with the materials of music. In play, the outcome is never predetermined. Try free improvisation from time to time. Listen to everyone else, and solo only when the coast is clear. Wait your turn. Then play only as long as your idea requires. Comment occasionally. Otherwise, subside into an ostinato in your low range until you have another chance.

## V. A Few Basic Principles

It is well to remember at the outset of teaching that human beings made music for millennia before any sort of musical notation was invented.

Most recorder instruction books for beginners start with the G pentachord. Immediately, this demands the awkward backtracking maneuver from B to C' and the quite illogical thumb-only high D immediately thereafter. And on top of these complications, the right-hand fingers have nothing to do for weeks or months on end, so that hand wanders into odd positions that take far too much time to correct later on.

Starting with either G or C Pentatonic, on the other hand, matches the technique of the recorder and avoids the use of any cross-fingerings until F Pentatonic is introduced. By then, finger control is secure enough that muscles can easily manage the multiple finger movements involved in producing F of F# or Bb.

With the introduction of F, the diatonic realm of C and related modes opens up, since all the notes are already under the fingers and need only be combined in E-F, B-C' progressions to complete the scale. With F# and Bb, the diatonic scales based on G and F are accessible, along with the inexhaustible repertoire of their major and minor modes. (See *My Recorder Reader* 3, Brasstown Press, for specific information and instruction.)

The remaining chromatic fingerings are introduced one by one, as needed. There's no hurry at all, if we choose to follow the Orff progression. That is what I have done in my three "RIT" books. (See *Recorder Improvisation and Technique, Books One, Two and Three,* Brasstown Press.)

I want to stress that the logic of the Orff sequence is enormously clarified and reinforced when we follow a parallel teaching approach to the recorder, instead of treating Orff as an entirely separate discipline, as is too often the practice. There is no contradiction between what we are teaching in recorder instruction time and the Orff techniques and repertoire we teach in ensemble time. Each amplifies the other, securing Orff's carefully thought-out sequence. It also avoids the usual confusion of scales and modes and changing accompaniment styles that happens, under so much time pressure, in short graduate-level summer workshops.)

This is what I can recommend for specific age groupings:

- For *young children,* I like to begin with the tetrachord of D E G A. It's a good singing range for them, and both hands are required to play. Limited-range playground chants and folk songs with various tonal centers may be introduced rapidly, as well as tunes improvised by both the children and the teacher. (See *My Recorder Primer*, Brasstown Press.)

- For *third and fourth grade children* I prefer to start with repertoire in G Pentatonic and its related modes. This gets the right hand into play as soon as possible and, again, by far the majority of our folk songs are in the plagal position, with the final in the middle of the range – NOT, as in Orff-Schulwerk Volume I, in authentic position with the final at the top or bottom. (See, *My Recorder Reader 1*, Brasstown Press). I next move on to C and F Pentatonic before hexatonic and diatonic are introduced.

- For *upper grade children, young people, and adults* who are learning both to play the recorder and basic Orff methods, I like to begin with C Pentatonic. It makes obvious the parallel sequence between Volume I and the presentation in my *RIT* books. These classes usually move so fast that the problem of a misplaced right hand doesn't arise. Also, using C Pentatonic makes the repertoire from the Schulwerk and supplements immediately accessible for students.

—

*A version of this essay first appeared in The Orff Echo Volume 24 Issue 1 [1991] and Volume 24 Issue 2 [1992]. Reprinted with permission from The Orff Echo, the quarterly journal published by the American Orff-Schulwerk Association.*

# 10 HOW TO INTRODUCE THE ORFF ENSEMBLE

*IMC explains how a teacher can bring children naturally into creative ensemble playing.*

I like to begin my ensemble sessions with a variety of improvisational exercises on the bar instruments, whatever the age and stage of the class. Set up the pentatonic scale you want to use, and ask the children to count off into teams by 4, 6, or 8. Each person will play a melody as long as it lasts and finish with a tremolo on the last note, very quietly, as a signal for the next player to start his or her own melody. When the last player has finished, everyone plays a gradual crescendo on the tremolo and ends with a gradual diminuendo until the sound disappears.

Then it's time for the next team to take a turn.

There are no other rules. But its wise for you to start off each group in the beginning, and if someone gets carried away and goes on too long, you can remind everyone to keep their tunes in proportion to others in the set.

After class proficiency has improved, you can make some suggestions about picking up an idea from someone who has already played, playing stepwise tunes, or using skips or repeated notes. Propose a lively tune, or a sad one, or a lullaby, or a march.

As everybody listens more and more attentively, improvisations will improve in musicality, becoming more related to each other and more aesthetically satisfying.

Inexact Echoes

Another technique I like to use from the very beginning is an inexact echo. I ask the class to play back whatever I play in the same rhythm, the same technique, and same length as I do, but without worrying about the same notes.

If I play stepwise figures, they do, too. If I play two notes at a time in parallel movement, they do, too. If I play figures with repeated notes, then they do that, too. In this way they build up their own technique and their aural acuity and memory, and soon some of them will be matching my notes as well – at least part of the time.

Line up the student players at the Alto Xylophone (AX). Facing the line of students, Teacher chooses one note on AX and plays a short pattern, alternating hands. When it is his/her turn, the student echoes the teacher's pattern on AX. The other waiting students patsch the pattern on their favorite knee, and sing the note on the chosen pitch. The player then goes to the end of the line and patsches the next patterns, while the others move up into line at the AX to echo the Teacher, until all have had a turn.

To Teacher: keep changing the note and rhythm, but keep it short.

Later, you can expand this exercise to use all the bar instruments available, letting students choose their own note in the C Pentatonic setup.

## Exact Echoes

After inexact echoes are within the class's grasp, I introduce exact echoes, where students match my pitch, along with the rhythm, technique and length I play.

Variations:

- Playing on knees (patschen).
- Using several bar instruments, students echo the exact music simultaneously.
- Transfer the echo-play to other instruments.

## Question+Answer Play

The Teacher plays the same short melodic Question. In turn, each volunteer student plays an Answer with an improvised phrase.

Variations:

- Line up to play on the same instrument.
- Play on all the available bar instruments in the classroom.

## Ostinato Patterns

Begin with alternating octaves on C's, on G's

- Play repeated open fifths
- Then introduce stepwise patterns, alternating hands
- Add ostinati in combinations with other music, for example, a So-Mi chant to a familiar rhyme.
- A *So-La-Mi* setting of a rhyme with Hand Sign singing
- Teacher's solo improvisation on Soprano Recorder (SR)

## Building The Carpet Of Sound

---

*The patterns are not interrupted again, and again, but continue quite independently of the phrase breaks in the melody itself. There are no holes in the Carpet of Sound! The patterns provide a forward impetus at every phrase break in the melody as the rhythm continues its hypnotic movement into the next phrase, and the next. This is how rhythmic security is built in the Orff Approach.*

IMC, "THE MAGIC CARPET," IN *MAKING IT UP AS YOU GO*, BRASSTOWN PRESS.

---

The following guidelines help to construct the momentum and support of an effective Carpet of Sound.

AXIOM

- The fewer voices, the more each can do; the more voices, the less each can do.

RULES

- NO HOLES IN THE CARPET! Ostinati are what keep it all moving; make sure they overlap the spaces between melodic phrases and maintain continuous forward momentum.
- The phrasing is in the melody, not in the accompanying ostinati.

## Goal

- Strive for rhythmic contrast between parts, as well as contrasting timbres, and complementary ranges.

To begin, build the layers as follows:

1. Establish the meter and tonality in the lowest voice.
2. Add middle range ostinato, either Alto Xylophone (AX) or Alto Metallophone (AM), as appropriate.
3. Add an upper pattern that either reinforces the melody or complements it sparingly.
4. Add appropriate unpitched percussion.
5. Add improvised melody (or)
6. Add chosen melody, sung and/or played + combined resources.

As an illustrative exercise, consider the following:

- For an A-G-E melody, build layered ostinati in *La* Pentatonic on A and E
- Ask a volunteer to lead Hand Sign singing over the instruments.
- With sets of four volunteers, add Q+A playing on Alto Glockenspiel (AG).

For another exercise, try these ideas:

- Build layered ostinati on G and D in G Pentatonic for a lively improvised dance.
- With volunteers for Question and Answer (Q+A) play on Soprano Xylophone (SX) and AX (or other instruments of your choosing)

- With Pass-It-On, each person improvising in turn, until the melody is finished. (The insecure can simply "pass" until they're ready to participate.)

Then ask yourselves some questions. What happened after each exercise? As you'll see, the possibilities are endless. Here are some ideas to get you started:

- What's needed next as you build the Carpet of Sound?
- Do the patterns fit together? Is there rhythmic tension among the parts?
- Are there any "holes in the carpet" that need to be filled?
- What tone color should we choose next?
- Do we need to add any unpitched instruments? For emphasis or color? Or for dramatic effect?
- What is the best choice for a solo above the ensemble?:
- Do we want to add Hand Sign song improvisation?
- What about solo improvisation on SX or AX?
- What about Question+Answer play on two Glockenspiels?
- Do we want to include a magical poem and make this a "Sound Setting" or "Klang-Ostinato" piece?
- Is this an overture for a mini-opera on a familiar folk tale?

Keep in mind, in all exercises, whether with adults or children, *all soloists must volunteer*. No one is expected to improvise or solo until he or she feels ready to do so. Especially with young ones, all criticism must be impersonal, or you can kill for life a child's impulse to play with the wonderful materials of music.

## Resources and Inspiration

Basic ostinato parts can be found in the Orff repertoire, and can be taught by rote to classes of children as well as adults. Introduce simple ostinato parts, for example, #8 from Keetman's *Erstes Spiel am Xylophon*, Schott 5582.

Gunild Keetman's two books, *Spielbuch für Xylophon* I (Schott 5576) and II (Schott 5557), were originally published in 1965-66, long after the five volumes of the Schulwerk. (*n.b.* The early editions were numbered 1a and 1b, instead of I and II.) Here Keetman explores the realm of the pentatonic, using all possible modes without half steps in delightful pieces for two Alto Xylophones. In her endnotes, she suggests doubling the parts with Soprano Xylophone (SX) and Bass Xylophone (BX) and developing the ostinato accompaniments for larger ensembles.

In the Book I, the earliest pieces are for one hand at a time – as children naturally play. Later, she indicates the sticking for alternating hands quite conscientiously, while suggesting that each child work out their own. Book II includes a few examples of pentatonic scales with half steps and the stimulating possibilities. It also contains many more delightful ostinato pieces, many of them considerably easier than all but a few in Book I. The ostinato patterns are, as usual, astonishingly varied and ingenious.

One characteristic of Keetman's style that always delights me is her skillful use of dissonance. There are lots of seconds in these pentatonic arrangements, and even more frequent dissonances in the major and modal diatonic scales that were used in the later Schulwerk volumes. Another characteristic of these pieces is that most of them are not anchored to a tonic (or dominant) drone, but use widely moving contrasting patterns to support the melodies. This nicely illustrates my axiom: "The fewer instruments, the more each can do; the more instruments, the less each can do." It is always interesting to add a tonic drone in the bass and compare the effect with and without it.

My own three books available from Schott, *Recorders with Orff Ensemble, Vols. 1, 2, 3*, also provide a wide range of pentatonic pieces, as well as hexatonic and diatonic examples. Most of them are in ostinato style: sometimes with a hand drum, a single accompanying instrument, three or four instruments, or a large ensemble. There are also several composed for multiple recorders with unpitched percussion accompaniment. As with Keetman's pieces, most of them are intended for use in movement as well.

—

*This article was previously unpublished.*

# 11 PRACTICING SOME NEGLECTED ENSEMBLE TECHNIQUES

*Never satisfied with the standard fare, IMC exhorted her students and colleagues to expand their reach. She reminds teachers and ensemble musicians about additional techniques for developing arrangements of existing compositions, and for creating new ones.*

Following are some of my favorite techniques that add interest to settings and arrangements of music for the Orff ensemble. In my opinion, we don't use them enough. Try these ideas as inspirations for your own.

I. Use the Entire Orff Ensemble

Use the ensemble on an improvisation in the Aeolian Mode. Then add:

• Group vocal improvisation over layered ostinati

• Solo recorder improvisation

• Q+A play with chosen resources

## II. Make your Own Klang-Ostinato (Soundscape) Setting

Set a short, magical folk rhyme or poem for speech choir using unpitched percussion for punctuation and atmosphere. Consider including movement as well.

Examples:

> *A black fairy flew,*
> *Played nicky nicky noo*
> *On my silly poo,*
> *And I'm off to tell the King*
> *That Babbin's fallin'.*

EXCERPTED FROM *CHICKEN LITTLE*

> *Turvey, Turvey, clothed in black.*
> *With silver buttons all down your back,*
> *One by one and two by two,*
> *Turn around, and that will do!*

Build the ensemble using a few carefully chosen bar and unpitched percussion instruments to support the spoken text and set the atmosphere.

Examples:

> Wild Day at the Shore
> *Upward a gull, out toward a tern,*
> *Upward and outward and seaward,*
> *Inward the wind, downward the waves,*
> *Inward and downward and leeward;*

*Wind, waves, and sky*
*Gull, tern, and I.*

UNKNOWN

November Night
*Listen,*
*With faint dry sound,*
*Like steps of passing ghosts,*
*The leaves, frost-crisped,*
*Break, from the trees*
*And fall.*

ADELAIDE CRAPSEY (1878-
1914)

## III. Arioso Settings

In the opera, an arioso is more melodic than recitative, and shorter and more informal than an aria. In arioso technique, one or more soloists improvise freely over a small, rather static ensemble. Try having the soloists sing the names of team assignments, for example, (between statements of the *tutti* section):

Team 1: Weeds or wildflowers
Team 2: Trees
Team 3: Birds or beasts

The melody may be sung phrase by phrase by a soloist, echoed by the group, led by Hand Signs for all to sing, or worked out independently by each group along with their solo section, and then shared. Repeat words or lines and insert instrumental bridges, as you choose.

IV. Paraphony

The Medieval technique of paraphony, the use of parallel harmonic lines, often at intervals of thirds and sixths, above and below the melody, is characteristic of some of the most memorable pieces in the Schulwerk Volumes. It is, of course, readily applicable to newly composed music in the classroom.

Examples from the Schulwerk include:

- Parallel fifths and octaves e.g., Volume IV page 72: Unto Us a Child Is Born
- Parallel thirds and sixths: Volumes II and IV: Voici le Noel
- Triads in root position: Volume IV pages 88-9
- Triads in first inversion: Faux-bourdon or Fa-burden: Volume IV page 50
- Triads in open position: Volume IV pages 51, 117

Experimentation with parallel harmonic lines in your own and classroom compositions and arrangements can yield delightfully rewarding music.

V. Umterzen

"Umterzen" was Carl Orff's name for playing around with thirds. Often known in English as "Decoration of the Third," this historic technique fills in and ornaments thirds over parallel open fifths. It provides wonderful preparation for Renaissance ornamentation.

Departing from the tried and true methods of arranging music for your classroom will enliven your lessons and expand your choices. Your students and you will be the richer for it.

—

*This essay was previously unpublished.*

# 12  MASTER CLASS: COMPOSING AND ARRANGING FOR THE ORFF CLASSROOM

*This outlined course of study in fifteen assignments (I-XV) will prepare teachers for a lifetime of composing and arranging using the Orff Approach. Schulwerk references are to the Murray Volumes.*

Before starting on the first assignment, note the following, for use through this course. These are basic guidelines that will apply here and more generally to composing and arranging in the Orff style.

1. Establish the tonal center with a drone in the lowest part. The drone may use the final, its dominant, or both.
2. Use rhythmic contrast between instruments. (Except at the very beginning stage, when it may be necessary to reinforce the pulse or basic rhythm of the words in a song.)
3. Choose the instruments to reinforce the mood and atmosphere of the melody you're arranging or composing.
4. Assign attractive patterns to each instrument so that you make the best use of its possibilities and so each part is clearly heard.

5. Avoid parallel fifths and octaves (except in paraphony), especially between the melody and the bass.

6. Use contrary motion between parts as much as possible. When inventing an ostinato, be sure to keep the Carpet of Sound intact across phrase-breaks in the melody. An ostinato is not end-stopped, like a phrase, but camouflages the phrase-breaks by carrying the rhythmic movement across the necessary breath into the next phrase and the next. *No holes in the carpet*, please!

7. Choose your texts with the utmost care. Whatever is taught in this style will be remembered all through a child's life. Only the best from our folk heritage and the realm of children's literature is worth using in depth, as we do in the Orff Approach.

8. NEVER take a motif from the song or melody you're setting to use as an ostinato, since it will disappear into the tune whenever they coincide. The only exception to this rule occurs when the motif is used contrapuntally.

9. Choose your folk songs and dances and compose your own melodies with the greatest care, so that they are at the best stage for what you intend to use them. Pentatonic songs, for instance, must avoid strong harmonic emphases to be appropriate for Bordun-Ostinato setting.

Not all pentatonic songs or tunes are appropriate for our use. Some are simply "gapped majors" with too much emphasis on the fifth or the second degrees. Similarly, when the full diatonic scale is used with Bordun-Ostinato accompaniment (as in Volumes II and IV, Part I) the tunes must be basically Ionian in major keys (Volume II). In Aeolian, Dorian, and the other modes, the tonic must be paramount, with tones of the tonic chord falling on almost every accent. (E.g., "The First Noël")

At the shifting chord stage the tunes must be carefully chosen to fit this specialized technique, with clearly implied chordal patterns outlined in the melody. (E.g., "The Drunken Sailor")

## I. Speech Exercises

Choose a folk rhyme that would appeal to primary children and lends itself to rhythmic play. Counting-out rhymes, weather prophecies, charms, and nonsense rhymes are particularly suitable.

Write at least five different rhythmic versions of the rhyme itself with the rhythmic notation over the words, as in Schulwerk Volume I. Experiment with various meters; extensions through repetition of words or phrases; the use of augmentation; shifting meter within the rhyme (perhaps from 3/4 to 6/8); mixed meter; dynamics; and vocal timbre.

Choose one version to develop in each of the following ways, with a particular class in mind, using

- Body percussion ostinato reinforcing the pulse
- Body percussion patterns doubling the word rhythm
- Independent rhythmic ostinato pattern(s) using either body percussion or unpitched percussion
- Independent speech ostinati
- Both speech and rhythm ostinati

NOTE: Be sure to avoid using words or phrases from the rhyme itself as ostinato figures, since they vanish into the rhyme when they coincide, leaving large holes in your Carpet of Sound.

## II. Rhythm Instruments Exercise

Use unpitched percussion instruments (sparingly and with careful discrimination) to set the mood of an imaginative short poem or folk tale that would appeal to primary children. Work out your own notation for the rhythm instruments for the class to follow in a Sound Prelude, Accompaniment to the spoken poem or story, and a Postlude. The instruments are to be used for punctuation and dramatic effect, not as a continuous accompaniment in this case.

Teach the poem through echo-play until the children know it by heart, or tell the story a time or two for spontaneous movement or dramatic play before attempting your arrangement in class, both to save time and to be sure that the material strikes fire with the children.

### III. From Speech to Song

Find a short poem that appeals both to you and to children, and set it in each of the following three ways:

- As a speech exercise with speech ostinati and/or vocal sound accompaniment.
- As speech + rhythm accompaniment, using body percussion and/or unpitched rhythm instruments.
- Set the stage and scene with speech and rhythm patterns both before and during the poem itself. Use solo voices, small groups at different pitch levels, *tutti* sections, dynamic contrasts, specific timbres or ranges as seem appropriate.
- Using only A, G, and E, compose a tune that approximates the natural inflections of speech and add a simple Bordun accompaniment (limited to tonic and/or fifth) with either C or A as the tonal center. Add not more than 1 rhythm instrument and 1 melodic ostinato that a particular class could do. Or choose two ostinato patterns, one for all the woods, the other for all the metals. Take care that they are appropriate to those families; or one for the high

instruments, the other for the lows, so that all the bar instruments will be in use.

Write your composition in score, as in OS Volume I.

## IV. Question+Answer Phrases Exercises

Compose a series of Question+Answer phrases in 2/4, 3/4, or 6/8 meter, using only body percussion:

- Write out at least four examples, correctly notated as in Vol I, pages 84ff. or on staff paper, with:
- Stamps on the bottom line, Left foot with stem down, Right foot with stem up;
- Left knee on second line,
- Right knee on middle line with stems indicating which hand is to play;
- Claps on the fourth line, and
- Finger-snaps on the fifth line, again indicating which hand is to play if the movement is not in unison.
- Transfer two Q+A phrases to appropriate rhythm instruments, using standard notation, as in Volume I Part II.
- Transfer two others to the bar instrument of your choice, using only C D E G (A).

## V. Rhythm Piece with Accompaniment

Compose a Rhythm Piece over a body percussion ostinato, as in Volume I, pages 62-63.

- Transfer your rhythm piece to unpitched percussion instruments, and revise the accompaniment if necessary to fit the new instruments.

- Work out simple movement patterns for each part that could be assigned to small groups, and plan how you would put your rhythm piece together in a primary classroom.

## VI. The Pentatonic Modes

Write out the five pentatonic modes in the F Pentatonic setup: *Do* Pentatonic, *Re* Pentatonic, *Mi* Pentatonic, *So* Pentatonic, and *La* Pentatonic. Letter names will do.

- Which of them are AUTHENTIC? (With the final at the top and bottom of the scale.)
- Which are PLAGAL? (With the final in the middle of the scale.)

Improvise on Alto Xylophone with *La* as the final in the C setup, using the range from E to E´.

Switch to *Re* Pentatonic, with D as the final.

Switch again to *Do* Pentatonic, from C to C´.

What difference does it make to the character of the melody whether it's authentic or plagal?

## VII. *La* Pentatonic Exercise

Compose a little march for Soprano Recorder using C D E G A with *La* (A) as the tonal center.

- Work out and write down at least three movement variations, with specific locomotor movements in mind, changing the meter, tempo, dynamics, accompaniment, and the melody itself as needed. E.g., Skipping, Running, Skating, Rocking, Jumping, Whirling, Slinking, etc.

- Find an American folk song in *La* Pentatonic with a limited range. Arrange it simply for a specific class to play. Use no more than two bar instruments and two rhythm instruments in your setting, and notate it as in Volume I, Part III.

Using the notes of the F Pentatonic scale, work out a simple instrumental piece that a particular class of yours could do by Christmastime in *La* Pentatonic. E.g., Assign a simple rhythmic pattern to 2 timpani or hand drums:

- Traveling D – A – D´ Bordun in half notes on Alto Metallophone (AM) or Bass Metallophone (BM)
- Scale pattern on Alto Xylophone (AX) in quarter notes
- A, G half notes on Soprano Glockenspiel (SG) at the beginning of each bar, first low, then high
- Simple pastoral melody on Soprano Xylophone (SX), Alto Glockenspiel (AG), or Soprano Recorder (SR).

## VIII. Arrangement Exercise

Choose a simple American folk song or carol to arrange for your third or fourth graders. Use body percussion, not more than two Rhythm instruments, not more than three bar instruments, and a cello or bordun on a tonic drone, as appropriate.

- Use solo or small group sections for contrast with *tutti* sections if you wish.
- Include an Introduction, Interlude between repetitions, and Coda.
- Keep the patterns simple, but with good rhythmic contrast between parts.

SUGGESTED SOURCES

Seeger, *American Folk Songs for Children*, Doubleday

Seeger, *American Folk Songs for Christmas*, Doubleday

Seeger, *Animal Folk Songs for Children*, Doubleday

Bradford, *Sing It Yourself*, Alfred Music (A large collection of American Pentatonic songs)

Erdei and Komlos, *150 American Folk Songs*, Boosey and Hawkes

Carley, *My Recorder Reader Books 1-2-3*, Brasstown Press


## IX. Recorder Tunes for Movement

In *Do, La, Re,* and *So* Pentatonics in the G Pentatonic setup, work out unaccompanied melodies for movement on your Soprano Recorder.

- Write at least one tune in each pentatonic mode. Indicate the movement you have in mind and the appropriate tempo and dynamics in each case. Mark any necessary articulation so it won't be tiresomely "Da, da, da-ing" along. Try them out with your classes during movement time without telling the children how to move, and see if the music speaks to them. If not, revise as necessary.
- Transpose at least one tune to each of these pentatonic scales: F-G-A-C-D | G-A-B-D-E | D-E-F#-A-B | B-C-D-F-G. (Notice that all of these can be played on the diatonic bar instruments.)


## X. Dance in G Pentatonic

Compose a Dance in A B A form, with the A section In *Do* Pentatonic and the B section in *Re* Pentatonic. Assign the accompaniment for A to one group; for B to another, using whatever resources you need. Keep it at a third or fourth grade level.

## XI. Canon Exercise

Choose a saying, rhyme, or short poem that lends itself to canonic treatment in 2 to 4 parts:

- Arrange it as a Speech Canon, with or without body percussion, speech, or pitched percussion ostinati.
- Compose a simple pentatonic tune for your text that will work as a two-part canon. Use as much or as little accompaniment as seems appropriate. Write it out in score. See Volume I, pages 24, 32, 91, 131ff.

## XII. Rondo for Recorder Exercise

Compose a Rondo for yourself to play on the recorder over accompanying ostinato patterns played by children in your classes, using no more than three bar instruments and two rhythm instruments in each section in whichever pentatonic scale you wish.

- The Rondo theme should be in *Re* Pentatonic, perhaps over Bass Xylophone (BX) bordun, Alto Xylophone (AX) and Alto Glockenspiel (AG) ostinati.
- Section B in *La* Pentatonic with Hand Drum (HD), claves, and Bordun of your choice
- Section C in *So* Pentatonic, plus Tenor Recorder (TR) and 2 bar instruments.
- Section D in Q+A, Q+A form in *Do* Pentatonic, with the Questions given by you or a volunteer and the Answers improvised by volunteer soloists, either singing or playing Soprano Xylophone (SX) or Alto Glockenspiel (AG) over Bass Xylophone (BX) or Guitar drone. Remove the

unnecessary bars from the instruments before the children start to improvise. Write in your final score the best of the children's improvisations.

NOTE: Be sure to start each new section with the new accompanying patterns, usually introducing one at a time until they are together to your satisfaction. Keep the contrasting episodes both simple and essentially different in both sound and character from the A section.

- Keep a particular class in mind, and try out your Rondo with pupils or colleagues.
- Work out movement for the A section and one other episode, allowing solo or partner improvisation elsewhere, or a small group form worked out in class.

## XIII. *Far and Few* Exercise

Work out three different arrangements of Edward Lear's "Far and Few" from *The Jumblies* in his famous *Nonsense Book*:

1. For Kindergarten or First Grade, with a *So-Mi* tune over BX Drone, AX or SX scalewise moving ostinato, and a triangle for punctuation.
2. For mid-year second grade, with a *La* Pentatonic tune using *So, La, Mi*, (and *Do'* if necessary), with instrumental Introduction and Coda.
3. For third or fourth grade, make up a tune in *Re* or *So* Pentatonic, with up to four bar instruments and one or two rhythm instruments to add color and punctuation. Include:
   - Optional Introduction and Coda
   - Body percussion pulse Rhythm instrument ostinato
   - Movement

NOTE: Start with speech exercises if you wish, plus speech ostinati.

In 3. above, use more of the Lear poem over sound ostinati, if you choose, reserving the accompanied melody for the refrain above. Or say the rest of the poem yourself over a quiet body percussion accompaniment by the children, or a solo ostinato accompaniment to play yourself.

## XIV. Using Other Pentatonic Scales

Work out and notate complementary ostinato patterns for:

- BX, AM, and SG in D-E-F#-A-B pentatonic, with D as the tonal center or FINAL. Then use A as the tonal center.
- Cello (Vc) or Bordun, AX and AG in Bb-C-D-F-G pentatonic, with G as final.
- BM, 2 Timpani, and SX in G-A-B-D-E pentatonic with E as the tonal center.

Improvise melodic Questions for individual students to answer as you carry a Soprano Glockenspiel (SG) around the class. Write out the two best Q+A pairs over the ostinati you worked out.

Using these, or similar combinations of instruments and ostinati, improvise on your recorder over the ensemble, then lead the class with Hand Signs while they sing or play recorders. Or let volunteers from the class take turns improvising melodies on the bar instruments of their choice. Or choose a text for a song and let the class work out a melody together in the appropriate pentatonic mode.

## XV. Storytelling in Recitative over Bordun Accompaniment

Choose a favorite folk or fairy tale with a particular class in mind, and work out recitative in their best range, using only three notes from the pentatonic scale of your choice.

Decide on the reciting tone on which most of the narration will be sung, in natural speech rhythm. Move to a higher pitch only for emphasis and to a lower pitch just before the cadence at a comma, semicolon, or period. Use rhythm instruments for color and punctuation to be played only as you direct. Assume that you would be the narrator yourself, at least initially, and play your own accompaniment.

If you choose a story with a recurring response, the class can work it out either in recitative style or in a mini-aria or song, as seems appropriate. (The Gingerbread Boy – "I am a gingerbread boy, I am...." or Three Billy Goats Gruff – "I'll huff and I'll puff and..." would be good examples.)

- Include appropriate instrumental interludes that you and your class could play, with a layered ensemble supporting the melody and simple "arias" to be sung by characters in the drama, accompanied by ostinato patterns.
- Plan the appropriate mime or drama, and let the children participate at will until the soloists have been chosen.
- Compose a simple Prelude, Interludes as needed between scenes, and a Postlude. *Keep It Simple* so that your class can gradually take over these assignments.

NOTE: For preschool and primary children, you will probably need to simplify your assignment and simply *tell* the story over an ostinato that you play yourself, changing the pattern as the mood of the story changes, and inserting interludes for movement or changes of scene as the story requires, plus the suggested prelude and postlude. At this age and stage, it would be wise to keep the whole project as informal and spontaneous as possible while allowing the children to enjoy (1) dramatic play, (2) using rhythm instruments as above, (3) playing simple drones +/- melodic ostinato patterns to support the short "arias" or response songs required by the text.

Let different children assume the roles on different days and repeat the story as often as necessary to give most of the children a chance to participate as actors, "supers" (like sheep in Little Bo-Peep, for instance), singers, or players, as they choose, without attempting a public performance.

Invite parents for a demonstration instead. Otherwise the children will be worn out before the project is ready and the fun will evaporate.

The more improvisation the better! Only one or two set songs or pieces at the simplest level.

—

*This essay was previously unpublished.*

# 13  TEACHING MUSIC TO PRESCHOOLERS

*As much as she relished the challenges of working with adults and older children, IMC fostered a special love of materials and techniques that brought out the best in young children. Here are some of her thoughts, distilled from decades of teaching experience and literature review.*

## Some Preliminary Notes and Thoughts

Little children are very different from us.

Using the Orff Approach in the preschool setting requires adaptation. The original Schulwerk was for eight- to twelve-year-old students, and must be adjusted for preschool.

Think about how much Orff assumes at the beginning of Volume I of the Schulwerk. Many older children, well into the primary grades, would still be ill equipped to deal with those pieces.

So where do we begin? We begin with a multisensory approach, large muscle movement, bi-lateral movement, movement exploration, and finding the beat – both our OWN, and the common beat.

---

Unless they are moving, little children are not learning.

DEE COULTER

---

Keep in mind that the young child:

- Has a short attention span
- NEEDs to move
- Needs to alternate large muscle movement and concentrated activity
- NEEDs much repetition

Remember that, up to four years or perhaps older, the child is completely egocentric. Accordingly, it is VERY hard to wait, to take turns.

What do we make of this? We remember repetition, and keep repeating, but with a DIFFERENCE. We do the same activity but each time, for example, changing the ball from large to small to beanbag.

More considerations:

- Extend an activity with repetition
- Think "before and after" and build a sequence, then a whole story
- Add new props and characters to the story
- Add accompaniment – autoharp, rhythm instruments (one or two), bass bars, bass xylophone

- Vary the game or activity to make it more challenging – e.g. roll / bounce / toss / clap / catch
- Introduce both movement in place, and movement in space

**Speech Play** is wonderful with young children. Use it to cultivate skills including listening, singing, and playing – using body percussion as well as rhythm instruments. At first, play only at teacher's signals, for punctuation or color, for accents.

A single lesson can include movement and perception (for example, a listening song), speech play, and music time (repetition play, response song, activity song).

## Why Music for Preschoolers?

These days, we need to be ready to answer this question. Here are some of the many reasons for introducing preschoolers to music:

- It's fun!
- Music permits an instantaneous, personal emotional release. There's no "middleman," and the child has an immediate response.
- An early introduction to music provides musical training, including familiarity with elements like pitch, phrasing, melodic movement, scale, and harmonic patterns from our cultural traditions.
- Preschool music promotes social development and mental health.
- As experienced teachers already know, music contributes a "magic cement" for the group, encouraging a sense of community and shared purpose.
- Like early experiences with art, music opens doors to individual creative exploration.

- Flowing directly out of Speech Play, **Singing** takes place in and out of the classroom, throughout the world. The preschool teacher can use singing to cultivate tone matching, first with echoes, then calls (like "Who can see..." in a hiding game), "Who has...?" if an object is hidden.
- It is good practice to sing in head voice, closer to the same range as the children, and with the airier timbre more similar to theirs. This is especially true for teachers with lower-pitched speaking voices.
- Music with preschoolers builds in **Participation**, so that almost all children forget themselves and often, for the first time, enjoy free group play.

## What Music?

There's a wealth of material to choose from for inspiration. Teachers may select their favorite age-appropriate books and recordings – including recorded stories, folk songs, World music, and well-chosen "adult" recordings like marching bands or music for the ballet.

Of course teachers are free to use some actual **Instruments** too in the preschool classroom. When it comes to live music on instruments, consider the following:

- Use the piano sparingly, focusing on simpler textures and sounds. Piano, played with a light touch, can be useful to add variety, changing the rhythms and the accompaniment "feel."
- Rhythm instruments are welcome additions to the preschool classroom, including drum, triangle, tambourine, sticks; and later, cymbals, bells, maracas, etc.
- Use a drum to establish the rhythm for movement.
- Other possible instruments can include autoharp,

flutophone, bird whistles, toy trumpets and xylophones (those last two, for four-and-a-half- and five-year-olds).

## How Music for Preschoolers?

Putting these ideas together, I recommend starting with speech play on word rhythms, using the children's names, as well as favorite nursery rhymes. (*Poems to Grow On* by Mabel Chandler Duch, now out of print, is a treasure house of ideas.)

Then move on to poems, which can lead to songs, and later still, to dances.

With five-year-olds, introduce pitched instruments used for sound sketches, rather than for melody or harmony. For example, assign one or more volunteers to play toy trumpet on "The King of France" at specified places in the rhyme.

When using the piano for a class, keep it simple. Play fifths on the quarter-note beat; and half notes to accompany folk songs. Occasionally insert a short piano solo for another tone color.

The children themselves can begin using instruments. I like to allow free experimentation with rhythm instruments.

As teacher, the drum is a favorite place to start. I drum with movement.

As some children gain comfort and facility with a drum, try to combine patterns using two, then three, rhythm instruments.

Children can learn so much with a simple folk song, for example,

- Loud and soft
- Fast and slow
- Crescendo and diminuendo
- Accelerando and ritard

- Patterning for phrasing
- Five-year-olds will also notice contrast of timbres
- Some preschool children will perceive formal contrasts, identifying an A/B structure in a longer piece, for example, having a slow verse and rapid-paced chorus.

Again, remember to keep it simple. Even if you are fortunate to have many instruments available, don't use all of them.

A limited number of textures and timbres is more effective with young children.

Generally, for young children, the emphasis is on:

- Movement
- Speech play
- Rhythm training
- Listening games
- Singing
- Activity songs and games

Children learn and grow so much through movement, which involves all of these:

- Body exploration
- Movement in place
- Locomotor movement
- Matching space and time
- Keeping a pulse. Research by Phyllis Weikart and others indicates how crucial this is to later use of language, and sense of equilibrium.

**It's essential to note that initial preschool movement and singing games should NOT involve patterns, or Right and Left.**

This means the children should have opportunities to move to the beat, both in place and in space, but without any set movement steps, group patterns, or solos.

As with early childhood education generally, it's crucial to match materials and activities to the child's developmental and skill levels. Pioneers like Maria Montessori and Jean Piaget, along with McVicker Hunt and other more recent theorists all point to these truisms.

## Speech and Rhythm for Preschoolers

With speech play and rhythm games, I like to begin by playing "Copycat," echoing the children's names.

- Copycat their names, for inflection, and for rhythm.
- Keep a beat going making rhythm patterns with claps, then patsch-clap combinations, and then with patschen patterns (both hands together, then alternating knees).
- Combine names into patterns, two at a time.
- Add rhythm instruments and/or movement, and later a *So-Mi* or *So-La-Mi* chant.
- When the class names are familiar, use categories like colors, trees, flowers, streets, towns, states, countries, lakes, etc.
- Simple rhymes for diction, rhythm, pulse, inflection and memorization; phrasing, timbre and FUN
- Add rhythm patterns to reinforce pulse. For instance, clap, then play the words on rhythm instruments; then step the pulse, and clap the words.
- Use dramatic play
- With the class, improvise a two-tone chant with Hand Signs and Alto Xylophone.

- Add rhythm instruments, rhythm patterns or Orff instrument accompaniment if needed – as simply as possible. Let the children help decide what (if any) instruments are most appropriate for this particular rhyme or chant.
- Try various spatial forms – *e.g.* sitting in a circle on the floor, sitting opposite a partner, walking (galloping) with a partner, etc., moving in a circle, moving in a line.

## Songs for Preschoolers

Teach a new song after sufficient preparation using melodic play with Hand Signs. Before you try to teach a tune, for the children to sing, get ready by copycatting the tones, rhythms, melodic motifs, and any problems the song presents.

Activity songs are for the *teacher* to sing. The class can act them out, move to them, and then sing along when they are ready. Activity songs include *Jim along Josie; Engine, Engine; New River Train*, and *Toodala*.

Introduce dramatic songs, too, for acting out, like *Over in the Meadow*, and singing games like *Here We Go Loop de Loo*, and *Punchinello* (in a circle formation around IT).

Little children may very different from us, yet they – like almost all grown-ups – share an innate delight when spontaneity and participation combine.

Prepare to enjoy yourselves!

—

*This essay was previously unpublished.*

# 14 CONCERNING RABBITS

*Spontaneity – even in front of an audience – was the thing. This is an early editorial IMC contributed to The Orff Echo. Several teachers wrote back in reply, agreeing wholeheartedly.*

In my experience, rabbits cannot be pulled out of hats unless previously put there by the magician. Yet the trick is met with amazement and delight by most of the audience, as if it were indeed pure magic.

Something of the sort seems to happen at all too many Orff workshops and conferences. What comes out is really only what the leader has put in ahead of time, yet when the pieces are brought out and fitted together in public, the result is general delight and amazement.

Admittedly, it's a lot easier to give such "demonstrations" when all the ingredients have been thoroughly prepared ahead of time and all that's needed is a public reassembly of the parts to show the process. Admittedly, it's a lot safer than trusting the audience to come up with some ideas to be incorporated both in the process and the final product. Admittedly, when we agree to do these public demonstrations we need to know what we intend to accomplish. Admittedly we need to determine plans, so that we can fall back on them if necessary. But nonetheless, it is, in my judgment, a complete travesty of the Orff Approach to present only pre-digested bits and pieces and to put these together in our public sessions, no matter how tempting this easy solution seems.

Personally, I'm tired of all these pre-cut, prepackaged performances – for that's what they are, performances. They have no relation to the actual teaching process that they pretend to represent, since all the ideas, all the techniques, all the development comes from the leader with no contribution from the group at all. Where is the interaction of class and teacher? Where is the improvisation, which is supposed to be one of the outstanding characteristics of the Orff Approach? Where is the immediacy of the creative experience? Can we dare to do what we proclaim, even when we're under the enormous professional strain of leading demonstrations and workshops in front of critical professional colleagues? Have we the courage to improvise in public? Do we trust our audience members enough to let them think and judge for themselves? Can we forgo sure-fire magic tricks for real teaching sessions?

It is not easy to surrender the obvious successes of the pre-packaged sessions that surround us. It is chancy, because some groups react much more creatively than others, and on these public occasions we have such limited time that it can be discouraging when the group response is slow and halting. But sometimes these very sessions that leave us, the leaders, feeling disappointed and let down will prove far more valuable to the participants. Those conspicuously "successful" sessions may have gone much too fast for the majority, and left them with nothing they could actually translate into their own teaching situations.

It is tempting for leaders to show how far ahead of the rank and file we are. People may marvel, yes, and applaud us and rally 'round with unconcealed enthusiasm at the end of these sessions. But have we really given them anything they can use themselves? Have we demonstrated the principles and philosophy of the Orff Approach we believe in?

Or have we played it safe and put on a show? Have we simply pulled our own rabbits out of our own hats?

—

*A version of this essay first appeared in* The Orff Echo Volume 10 Issue 3 [Spring 1978]. *Reprinted with permission from* The Orff Echo, *the quarterly journal published by the American Orff-Schulwerk Association.*

## 15   THE NEXT TEN YEARS: A VIEW FROM THE EARLY DAYS

*In 1977, when AOSA was ten years old, IMC wrote this heartfelt plea to her colleagues. Happily, some of her concerns were addressed over the ensuing thirty-odd years. Her vision of a "Level 4" teacher training course remains relevant to this day.*

Nowadays colleges and universities around the country are vying with each other for distinction as centers for professional Orff training with their "certification courses." The music industry has decided that we're here to stay, not the passing fad they once thought we'd be. So the situation is very different from the spring of 1967 when the AOSA was organized by eight Midwesterners who shared a dream. Our dream has come to a considerable level of influence and stability in these ten years, but the problem of teacher training remains a major concern.

This is still, to my knowledge, only one undergraduate major in Orff available at any American college or university (Hartwick College, Oneonta, NY). There is still, in many Departments of Music

Education, a bare mention of the Orff approach. It is only after they graduate that students from these more conventional schools find out what they've been missing. In most undergraduate programs, the Orff approach is lumped together with other contemporary approaches – Kodály, Manhattanville, CMP, or whatever interests the professor – in a very cursory way. So it is still largely a *graduate* course of study that we're confined to, and very limited one at that.

We are anchored to the traditional summer one- or two-week workshop pattern for established teachers who need more credits for re-certification and/or advanced degrees.

At the introductory level, one-week workshops will always make sense, but there are still many one-week workshops at intermediate levels.

Most schools schedule two-week workshops in a sequence over at least two years.

Only one, as far as I know, offers three-week workshops with 105 hours of class over each of three summers. (University of Denver).

One, two, or three weeks, whatever it adds up to, is never enough. Even well-trained musicians take time to learn new skills, or new ways of teaching. And many of our students have had uneven backgrounds, with shaky training in music history and theory, for example, making our summer workshops extremely demanding. In these short summer courses, vast amounts of new materials are concentrated into a very short period of time.

Many leaders in the Orff movement are too preoccupied with existing programs to pay attention to our common problems and long-range plans. Perhaps the time has come to *make* ourselves take the time to think ahead to where we want to be in five years, in ten years.

Perhaps the time has come to dream again of new ways of accomplishing our ends without having to wait for the educational establishment to perceive our needs and respond to them. What can we do? Where do we go from here?

There are, it seems to me, five possible developments within the current educational framework, and one that need not wait for official institutional action:

1.  Perhaps some AOSA chapters can take the lead in trying to influence local colleges and universities to teach Orff on the undergraduate level in more than a superficial fashion. Some AOSA chapters have made a special effort to recruit student members in the last couple of years, and now these students are in a good position to insist on getting the kind of undergraduate Orff training they want and need.

2.  Local school systems and universities with strong extension departments can offer more long-term in-service Orff training courses in which teachers can meet regularly for instruction, exchange of ideas, and workshop activities under supervision. They'll be able to count on regular feedback as they go about their jobs from one week to the next, without the intensity of the summer workshops to contend with.

3.  Universities already interested in serious Orff training can limit their one-week Orff courses to the introductory level, where it makes good sense, and lengthen their Level 1 and Level 2 courses to at least two weeks and preferably three. Their administrators will come to realize that new techniques, such as our approach requires, take more time than standard lecture courses, to bring their students to any kind of adequate proficiency.

4.  More universities should be urged to follow the lead of the University of Denver and offer correspondence courses throughout the year in those areas that can be taught on an

individual basis, such as Arranging and Composing in the Orff style.

5. More universities should be urged to set up special training courses for classroom teachers alone, not simply permitting them to tag along in courses designed for music specialists, as is now generally the case. Unless we make the effort to train primary classroom teachers to handle the music in their own classrooms, as is done in England and Germany, music in the schools will never be much influenced by our small band of Orffers. Many classroom teachers have far more imagination in applying the techniques we've taught them than we do ourselves, with our narrower training. Classroom teachers are also free to use music and Orff techniques when the children need them, when a break in the routine is indicated, as we ourselves, with our tight schedules, are not.

6. We can begin to break out of the pattern of sequenced summer workshops, good as they may be, and experiment with new kinds of courses, quite outside the current format, to answer the needs that the sequenced courses still leave unsatisfied. I would like to see, for instance, a course for Orff specialists, experienced teachers who are graduates of the present courses. This course would concentrate on different areas from year to year, especially those that our short summer courses can never have the time to do adequately in the short time allotted.

Perhaps one year, Movement and Advanced Recorder; another year, Improvisation in all media, and Repertoire; another year, Voice training and Choral Techniques and Repertoire, and Arranging for the Orff Ensemble.

The curriculum could be constructed to satisfy the needs of the registrants and the special expertise of each year's faculty. In such a seminar, the exchange of ideas among the participants themselves, coming from different backgrounds and teaching situations, might prove the most valuable part of the whole undertaking. Such a seminar seems to me an urgent need for all of us once we pass the student stage.

Graduates of every course I know are very critical of what they consider the holes in their Orff training. They feel cheated, and very much aware of their own shortcomings.

They are not yet aware that all of us feel the same way, no matter how long and seriously we have been committed to the Orff approach. They don't yet know that no one ever *arrives*: we just keep getting a little closer to our goals in an approach to music that requires competence in so many areas.

We needn't stop after we've achieved the aims of basic Orff training. In fact, we ought to establish opportunities that challenge us to keep learning and improving. The kind of "Level 4" seminar I'm proposing here seems at least worth a try. Is anybody interested?

—

*A version of this essay first appeared in The Orff Echo Volume 9 Issue 3 [Spring 1977]. Reprinted with permission from The Orff Echo, the quarterly journal published by the American Orff-Schulwerk Association.*

# PART 4

## GENESIS OF THE ORFF GESTALT

**G**

*So*

# GENESIS OF THE ORFF GESTALT

*Orff-Schulwerk is always music plus – not just to be performed or listened to; but music to be made, shared, sung, played, danced.*

ISABEL MCNEILL CARLEY

# 16  ON PATTERNS IN A MUSIC GESTALT

*IMC's enthusiasm for brain research continued, especially as it began to suggest ways to improve music education. If these tended to be consistent with the tenets of the Orff Approach, well, so much the better!*

Psychologists tell us that human learning is largely a process of perceiving new relationships and then conceptualizing them as a larger "Gestalt," a whole. A gestalt, however, is more than the sum of its parts, being an integration of complex patterns of whatever size or medium. Indeed, the human brain is so eager to recognize patterns that it can perceive them even when they're not really there! That's not a problem with the wealth of Orff patterns, as they *are* there – patterns of speech, of rhythm, of movement, of song, and of instrumental accompaniment. Carl Orff seems to have understood the significance of pattern recognition in human thought and learning long before psychologists did the research to prove the point.

Consider, for instance, the simplest body rhythm movement patterns used in the earliest stages of Orff training. These may combine two alternating movements to reinforce the underlying pulse of a rhyme or a song, or add a repetitive rhythmic ostinato to a familiar playground chant. Consider in Speech Play how single words or short phrases are used as a repetitive first accompaniment. Consider how speech and movement reinforce each other in regular patterns as students are learning to keep a common pulse. Consider the large muscle kinesthetic patterns of the simplest borduns, or the intricate melodic ostinato patterns on the bar instruments. Consider the repetitive movement patterns our students enjoy in game-songs, play parties, and original movement improvisations.

All of these patterned activities are fun to do, no matter how repetitive, since they satisfy what appears to be an instinctive human urge for rhythmic movement. How wise of Orff to build on this natural joy in rhythmic, large muscle movement, instead of depending on the orthodox learning tradition, as others do! No, there is another way. We do not need to require the immediate visual coding and decoding of a complicated set of symbols, demands on a child's fine muscle control in pursuit of performing skills, and daunting trials for beginners on the sophisticated instruments of our Western tradition.

The gestalt out of all these patterns automatically inspires a great deal of practicing since student drill is built into participation in the ensemble. Technical skill develops as sensitivity to the ensemble grows – by actual playing, not in private practice sessions. The consistent, developmental practice of patterns permits the introduction of ensemble playing almost from the very beginning of music training. Then, as pattern is superimposed upon pattern, a rich texture of contrasting sounds and rhythms is created and a natural polyphony results. Melodies, too, are clearly patterned, with much repetition to make their memorization easy and their form clear.

Consider the ease of teaching and learning one short pattern after another. Everyone in the class learns every part and can perform any individual pattern. All hear the entire texture of both melody and accompaniment, whatever the part each may be assigned. Every student learns to trust his or her kinesthetic memory and to play the patterns "on automatic," once the technical problems have been mastered. This holds concentration on all the peripheral details that transform an exercise into a musical experience. This gestalt is the relation of one part to another, the balance within the ensemble, the dynamic pattern of the composition or improvisation, and the flight of melody over the Carpet of Sound on which it so comfortably rests.

Consider the success of improvisation built upon the hypnotic effect of the interrelated patterns of a delightful ensemble sound. Consider rhythmic movement and carefully dovetailed melodic patterns, the surest and most musical way of shifting our students into a relaxed, right brain state of mind. That is when their natural musicality can flourish, free from the judgmental, self-critical, destructive interruptions of their left brains. Such an ensemble of players supports individual ventures in improvisation that could never otherwise occur.

What other approach to teaching or learning music has ever dared make use of our elemental musicality in this way? The Orff Approach itself is a true gestalt, binding together delight in rhythmic movement, perception of repetitive patterns, recognition of familiar patterns in new contexts, the play of melodic motifs, and the ever-changing possibilities of the materials of music. And what other approach can elicit cooperative effort from a disparate group of students of different backgrounds and level of skill, bringing them into an ensemble where everyone's contribution is valued?

No other approach encourages the outstanding musicality of some students without indulging in a star system. No other approach builds character along with musical skills. Or provides an emotional outlet and support that may bring new self-esteem and peer recognition to those whose academic achievement falls well behind their musical talents. No other approach trusts teachers and students alike to make their own aesthetic judgments, to make their own music, to depart from the printed score and make their own unique variations. No other approach dares to encourage improvisation from the beginning, and provides the techniques and means of doing so. No other approach teaches music by allowing the students to play with the materials of music like a composer.

Only the Orff Approach does. Every other way is still bogged down in trying to teach skills that only a small minority are likely to desire or ever attain, and that because of parents who can afford private lessons. Only the Orff music gestalt lets musicality grow from delight in rhythmic movement and our joy in perceiving and performing patterns. Now we can teach music to children in our time as heirs of a groundbreaking advance in ideas. How fortunate we are.

—

*A version of this essay first appeared in The Orff Echo Volume 15 Issue 3 [Spring 1983]. Reprinted with permission from The Orff Echo, the quarterly journal published by the American Orff-Schulwerk Association.*

# 17 FIRST ENCOUNTERING GUNILD KEETMAN

*This lovely bit of memoir is slightly revised from "On Changing Your Life," in* Making It Up As You Go: Selected Essays, *Brasstown Press.*

I shall never forget my first encounter with Gunild Keetman. It was in the summer of 1962 in Toronto, the evening before the first Orff conference and courses held in North America. Apparently we both had the same idea – to go over to the University of Toronto campus, get the lay of the land, and check out the building where the meeting would be held the next morning.

I recognized her walking slightly ahead of me, but I was too shy to speak out. We separately continued our explorations, yet I was very much aware of her. Over twenty years earlier, during my time in Chicago, the best I could do was to read several provocative articles about the "Orff Approach" in professional magazines. Two German friends showed me copies of the first two volumes of *Musik für Kinder* in the German edition and also let me doodle on their alto xylophone and metallophone, brought back from abroad. With no notion of how to proceed, I was ready and waiting when the Toronto conclave was announced. Immediately, I decided to go.

The conference was my opportunity to find out about this whole business directly from Orff and his colleagues, since what little I'd seen was definitely not self-explanatory. I did think that the emphasis on ensemble from the beginning sounded like insightful psychology, since it's always more fun making music with other people than playing alone. Armed with little more than that, I rode up to Toronto from Indianapolis with Candace Ramsay, who was teaching Music Education at Ball State in Muncie, Indiana. I declared I was prepared to learn everything I could.

Fortuitously, I managed another personal encounter with Keetman at the conference. Somehow I had the nerve to give her a copy of my just-published first book, *Eleven Miniatures,* a collection of piano pieces for children. The next day, she stopped me in the hall to tell me that she and Dr. Orff thought my pieces were ideal for children!

The conference was extraordinarily stimulating. Standout events were Professor Keller's classes on arranging and composing in the Orff manner, with repertoire from Schulwerk Volumes II, III, and IV. He gave us advanced students a taste of repertoire and techniques well beyond the introductory level, so we were able to form a wider view of the entire approach. I remember writing my first Orff arrangement, a setting of Richard Chase's version of *Cock Robin,* and reading through and analyzing pieces from the brand-new Orff-Schulwerk books I had just purchased.

Recorder Ensemble sessions with Arnie Grayson, Mimi Samuelson, Isabel Shack, and a good bass recorder player from Montreal, name forgotten, were outstanding. I'd rarely met really good players before, so it was a singular treat.

I was also quite taken with Dr. Orff's lecture demonstration where he played recorded examples of the Orff-Schulwerk repertoire. These were by English children in Margaret Murray's classes, presenting examples of body percussion, speech play, songs and dances, all out of the first three volumes. It was my first chance to hear this repertoire performed by actual children. (Later, there were live demonstrations put on by Lois Birkenshaw's students and others.)

Among other notable events were Dr. Walter's stimulating lecture on the background and importance of the Orff Approach. His talk was eventually reprinted in *Orff Re-Echoes I*, and is a valuable resource. Also, Dr. Richard Johnston's stunning lecture demonstration used many of our North American limited-range folk songs and rhymes. These were convincing examples of what could be brought into the Orff Approach, and he put them in contrast to the limitations of what he referred to as the "gapped major" scale that dominates in Volume I.

Dr. Johnston's sessions underlined the need to study, analyze and collect relevant folk material from our own traditions. This is something I started to do as soon as I got back home. I wanted to build a pentatonic repertoire of folk songs for my own music classes. (Let me suggest that you do likewise. Or at least order Louise Bradford's wonderful collection, *Sing It Yourself: 220 Pentatonic American Folk Songs,* a nearly inexhaustible resource.)

Little did I know what attendance at the Orff conference and my fleeting encounters with Gunild Keetman would lead to. The experience propelled me beyond my initial interest toward a professional determination to study the Orff Approach in depth. I wanted to understand it thoroughly and use it if I could in my own music teaching, for I sensed this was a remarkable synthesis that looked to place music at the center of education as a whole.

By the fall of 1963, I would be in Salzburg, Austria, husband and younger daughter in tow, ready to start my classes at the newly opened Orff Institute. There I would discover what a truly marvelous teacher, musician, composer, and advocate for children's music education Keetman was. She and Dr. Orff opened a door and I went through it.

—

*Another version of this essay appears in* Making It Up As You Go, *Brasstown Press.*

# 18 IMPROVISATION MAKES IT HAPPEN

*IMC was at ease when she improvised. In later years, at the end of a workday, she'd often sit at the piano, eyes closed, and play whatever came to her. In the classroom, she could extemporize on recorder, bar instruments, percussion, and speech play. She encouraged her students – young and old, trained musicians, classroom teachers – so much so, that they came to trust themselves to improvise as well. The Keetman story she refers to here is recounted by IMC in "On Changing Your Life," in* Making It Up As You Go: Selected Essays, *Brasstown Press.*

What won me over to the Orff Approach in the first place was its emphasis on improvisation. I experienced this originally on the weekend sandwiched between two weeks of a course at a conference at the University of Toronto in 1962. Barbara Haselbach, Lotte Flach, Carl Orff, Gunild Keetman, and Wilhelm Keller were some of the featured presenters or speakers.

I'll never forget Orff's magical reading of his 1953 dramatic spoken piece, *Astutuli*,* which he gave in Bavarian dialect before the entire assembly. None of us likely penetrated the accent, and very few knew enough German to translate more than the occasional word. But we didn't need to. For Orff used his speaking voice as a musical instrument, changing timbre, range, tempo, and dramatic character. For me, at least, it was a revelation of the possibilities of musical speech and of living a vivid life in the inner meaning of language.

I'd never heard the Schulwerk repertoire before. During Gunild Keetman's general session, she suddenly asked for volunteers to improvise on the recorder. My adventure on stage with my friend Candace Ramsey is retold elsewhere. The lesson Keetman taught me, that first session with her, was significant: The obvious is only the first musical step.

At the end of her session, Keetman announced she would lead the entire audience in a pentatonic improvisation. We had come to this conference from all over North America. We shared in common little else than a curiosity to find out about the Orff Approach. Then Keetman told us that we were going to improvise with no rules, except to keep our singing in the pentatonic. There was no talk of form, nor solo-and-group nor Q+A fallbacks. Amazing. Impossible?

Yet following Keetman's gestures, the hall burst into song, as she played recorder above us. We were making music together. For me, that was the decisive moment. I knew this was what I wanted to do with the rest of my life, to make music born of language, instruments, and an elusive goal that I'd been pursuing in my own teaching: creative improvisation.

—

*This essay fragment was previously unpublished.*

---

* A 1953 film of Orff performing *Astutuli* appears on YouTube here: https://www.y-outube.com/watch?v=HogcJoRBiEw

# 19  THE INCLUSIVE ART OF MUSIC

*In this essay, IMC celebrates the multiple elements that make up an effective Orff education – speech, the instrumentarium, and improvisation, of course. She also recognizes the courage and dedication an effective teacher must bring to the process. The reward for all this hard work: The "kind of spontaneous combustion that occurs when an idea strikes fire and students transform like magic before our eyes."*

The Orff Approach requires speech play, movement, singing, and the use of rhythm instruments and specially designed melodic percussion instruments. Why? For good reason: to make from music an inclusive art. This is what music was as practiced in ancient Greece, as it exists to this day among primitive peoples, and as it will always be in the spirit of children's play. Participation in the playing of music becomes a paramount humanizing influence, and in education, develops a child's sensitivity to sounds, to the ensemble, and to other people through a cultivated and creative imagination.

## Using All the Elements

The Orff-Schulwerk repertoire is music *plus*. These pieces are not meant just to be performed or listened to, but to be remade, shared, sung, played, danced. By combining composition, creative invention, and immediate discovery, individual growth is nurtured, not only in terms of musical skill and understanding, but also with regard to human awareness. Sounds, speech patterns, and movement awaken us to the possibilities in even the simplest music material.

The unique, universal quality of these exercises stems from Orff's deliberate decision to limit them to what he called *Elementarmusik* – elemental music to be made by players themselves and played by heart. Though rooted in the historic, Western musical tradition, which he knew well, Orff's methods are not concerned with perpetuating that tradition, nor the conventional musical skills on which it depends.

Instead, he took compositional and scoring techniques of our ancestors that were thought outmoded and antiquated, and rejuvenated them – though other cultures with different traditions never gave them up. Thus in the Orff-Schulwerk, tunes are primarily monodic and diatonic, rhythm and melody dominate the texture, and harmony is either the result of simultaneous ostinati or monotonously simple and repetitive drones.

Orff claims three idiosyncrasies for his approach to music education: (1) use of speech; (2) use of the "Orff ensemble" comprised of glockenspiels, xylophones, metallophones, small timpani, triangles, cymbals, woodblocks, and drums of various sizes, supplemented by strings and recorders; and (3) emphasis on improvisation.

For most Americans the emphasis on movement and rhythm training is new as a basic part of musical education. (Orff is the first to admit his debt here to Jacques-Dalcroze.) Instruments, especially those designed for children, open up a new and magical world of sound.

Even very young children can make their own music in the their own way by emphasizing improvisation and ensemble. The ear is the guide, not the eye.

Much attention is given to speech training. At first, words are used as rhythm instruments – for color, for sound, for the beat. This leads directly to chant and to melodic improvisation, and indirectly to purely rhythmic word pieces that are often invaluable as mnemonic devices.

The results may appear both strange and musically disappointing to critical outsiders, as they can't understand the creative purpose or see the need for patience to encourage musical growth from the inside out. But this teaching method is superior to imposed stages dictated by theoretical training and notions of testable progress, or the doling out of prepackaged lessons in "creativity" from the class textbook. And, in the classroom, it is more successful with children.

Inclusive music is deliberately *not* designed for performance. No audience is implied, and you're completely missing the point if you want to judge on the basis of audience reaction. Your first question shouldn't be, "How could I use this in performance?" Participation is what's wanted, using the instruments we are all born with – our voices and bodies. As students grow in ease and technique, speech turns to song, body rhythms to percussion patterns, and free movement to dance.

It isn't easy to teach this way. It takes courage to do new things in front of a class, even of children. Meanwhile, our cultural idea of music as entertainment has seeped uncritically into too many schools. The aim of music education seems to be the cultivation of technical skills and performance ability, and that's no matter what noble and high-sounding ideals the professional groups express.

Any attempt at general music education for all has long been abandoned. In music programs, it is almost always students who have had private music training outside of school who survive long enough to be in the select performing groups of our high schools. Ordinary mortals were excluded "on evaluation" some time ago.

### Challenges for the Teacher

In the Orff Approach, teachers are called on to teach in a different way. Those with training that was more dance-oriented will bring a different perspective than those educated in music and child development. For students, moving from one style of teaching to another can be very confusing until they are prepared to make their own choices and find their own way forward. The Orff approach should help them resist the imposition of finished forms, whether in dance or music or spoken dramatic recitations, and not impose a fictitious orthodoxy based on a particular teacher's interests or educational background.

The same is true of learning recorder. Muscles take time to learn – much more time than our minds – and pressure to "follow the teacher" leads to tension and less skilled playing than the student is actually capable of. Student composition and arranging also need time to flower. Over a few weeks, how many assignments can even the most conscientious student do well?

We teachers also need sufficient time to function with competence. Time for our study and analysis of models in the Schulwerk. Time to find our own source materials. Time to do different arrangements and write compositions, and try them out with our students or colleagues.

That's a far cry from rushing to fulfill the letter of the administration's law with a hastily contrived class assignment, due tomorrow, or postponing the challenging aspects of the Orff program because the "students aren't ready." They *are* ready.

It may be the teacher's own insecurities and self-consciousness that need to be addressed. This can particularly be the case with improvisation, a basic principle of the Orff Approach, but often neglected in the classroom.

I've found that vocal training is almost totally passed over in most Orff workshops. Here again, teaching good vocal habits to children depends on an understanding of the range and development of children's voices, and on the teacher's own vocal skill. But other issues always seem more burning, and as one result, the choral repertoire in the Schulwerk is often ignored completely in the short Orff courses. Then, naturally, that repertoire suffers further neglect by the graduates we send forth to teach children.

Percussion technique, especially on the bar instruments, the hand drum, and timpani, also demands time for private practice as well as ensemble play. Yet the supplementary books written by Gunild Keetman for xylophones, timpani, and small percussion are largely ignored in our teacher training courses. Too often, it seems we have great Orff resources available, but there just isn't the time to use them.

## What Now?

Many people, teachers and students, hold back and play it safe, settling for doing what is on the printed page. They miss out on the freedom of invention and expression that can grow and flourish from simple beginnings in movement and improvisation.

They are confused by the appearance and presentation of the Orff-Schulwerk, its crowded pages in multiple volumes. They are unfamiliar with the timbre and technique of the Orff instruments and cannot imagine the sounds just from looking at a score.

They are confused by these Orff Approach books that seem to speak to many levels at once. They have no idea how best to use them. They feel the need for more accessible American material from our own folk traditions, but have no idea how to make them their own.

And then the big question: How can this new approach fit into our public school system?

Obviously our situation is completely different from that of European schools. There, Orff's ideas have already been widely accepted and adopted. In the German and Austrian schools and classes I have visited, the children were incredibly patient and polite. The authoritative German approach, however, can never be successful here.

As Americans, we have to assimilate Orff's ideas in our own ways. For example, the workbook methodology introduced in my own books could not succeed where children have never been encouraged to think for themselves, but only to respect authority and repeat what they've been told.

As teachers, we need a kind of spontaneous combustion that occurs when an idea strikes fire and students transform like magic before our eyes. Whatever they may choose to do, wherever they may go, children will always remember those special days in music class when their own ideas were accepted, developed, and used to create a precious experience.

Surely, this must be a paramount goal of any educational system, to make learning an unforgettable delight?

So, is anybody still interested?

—

*This essay was previously unpublished.*

# PART 5

## APPLIED ART IN ACTION

**A**

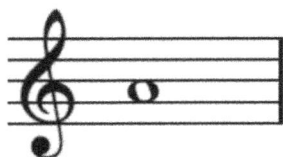

*La*

# APPLIED ART IN ACTION

*Tell me, I forget. Show me, I remember. Involve me, I understand.*

CARL ORFF

# 20  THE ESSENTIAL ROLE OF THE RECORDER

*IMC wrote this essay for the magazine of the American Recorder Society. She shares with aficionados the value of the recorder to music education in the Orff classroom. This new version includes additional manuscript text and examples not previously published.*

The recorder has been an integral part of the Orff Approach ever since Curt Sachs suggested to Carl Orff in the Güntherschule days that he add the recorder to his ensemble of pitched and unpitched percussion instruments. Today, all Orff teachers are expected to be able to play the recorder. They should play well enough to teach songs or instrumental melodies by rote; to improvise over student-played layered ostinato patterns; to lead with the more difficult solos in the Schulwerk class ensembles; and to encourage students to play the recorder well enough to tackle the wide variety of available repertoires. These include the basic five volumes of the Orff-Schulwerk and its many supplements, and the many American and other foreign publications for recorder and Orff ensemble.

Why this emphasis on the recorder?

Let me suggest the following reasons:

- It is the only melodic instrument in the Orff ensemble that can provide a legato line, akin to the human voice.
- It is one of three major melodic resources in the ensemble, and provides a welcome change of timbre, range, and tone quality from the glockenspiels and singing voices.
- It effectively doubles the voice an octave higher, reinforcing and enriching the melody, and is used effectively in descant song settings.
- It promotes music literacy with an approach that emphasizes rhythmic security and aural memory before cultivating reading skills.
- It is relatively simple to play. Inexpensive and widely available, it is nonetheless a real instrument, not pre-anything, and belongs to a family of instruments. As skills develop and other larger recorders are introduced, the world of chamber music opens for young players in an Orff Ensemble or recorder consort.
- It brings music history alive with the wide range of historical repertoire from the Middle Ages until today.

I find the very construction and technique of the recorder fit the Orff progression perfectly. We can begin with the pentatonic scales of C, G, and F, and their related modes, usually in that order, neatly avoiding the need for cross-fingerings. When hexatonic scales are introduced, separately adding *Fa* and *Ti*, they are already familiar. For example, when moving to C Hexatonic with *Ti*, the B is already familiar as *Mi* of the G Pentatonic scale; when moving to C Hexatonic with *Fa*, F is already familiar as *Do* in F Pentatonic. Once both hexatonics have been introduced, all the notes of the full diatonic scale are already known and need only be recognized and used. From there on, it is simply a process of "filling in the holes" to build whatever scales and modes we wish to use.

Since it is a *wind* instrument, the recorder demands a skillful use of articulation to make phrasing and musical form clear, particularly against the continuous layered ostinati of the ensemble. These ostinati are deliberately constructed to camouflage the natural breaks in the melody. When singing, we follow the punctuation of the words almost automatically, as we are accustomed to do when reading, whereas in playing the recorder, we must learn to understand musical style and form to communicate clearly.

The recorder is also the ideal instrument for melodic improvisation over the Orff Ensemble, as this combination is mutually flattering. The ensemble's underlying and continuous "Carpet of Sound" – to use Orff's phrase – will support and give confidence to improvising players that assignments in unaccompanied improvisation never could. The developing techniques of improvisation can be readily transferred to other instruments in the ensemble, but they are first and best cultivated with the recorder, since every child has one and doesn't have to wait for a turn at one of the bar instruments.

## The Role of Teaching Techniques

Let me shift attention to the teaching techniques that I believe are typical of a well-trained Orff teacher. These are techniques that I have employed myself and taught to other teachers for many years. So they have, at the least, withstood the basic test of educational pedagogy: practical use in the classroom.

Normally, children start recorder in the third or fourth grade, after they've had two or three years of Orff training – if they're lucky. The process begins with melodic echo-play on one or two notes. With young beginners, I like to start with G and E notes, so both hands are immediately in use; the right can't wander aimlessly, as often happens with conventional G pentachordal instruction. (With adults I'll start with second-octave C and A.)

I may ask the students to echo the rhythm and exactly match the length of my figure or phrase. Once this comes easily, it's time to insist on the exact tune and articulation.

For example, using a two-line staff:

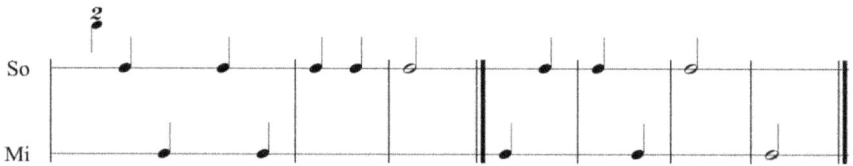

At first, the echo patterns are very short and rhythmically simple, for the whole class to respond to at once, but it's not long till the pattern lengthens, the range expands, and the rhythms get more complex. The teacher must be prepared either to repeat the pattern as often as necessary until it's right, or to go on to a new one with no interruption of the rhythm. Soon, the echoes are directed to each child in turn and tailored to that particular child's level so that success is almost guaranteed. When a child makes a mistake, it's understood that the whole class plays on the repeat so no one need be embarrassed. These improvisatory warm-ups are, of course supplemented with reading and learning pieces at the same level.

Each new note is introduced in the same way through "echo-play" and repeated until the fingering combination is secure with already familiar notes. Slurs, staccatos, double-tonguing, etc. are also introduced in echo-play before they are encountered in notation. That way each technique is already there before it's needed in repertoire.

As soon as the class echoes accurately and musically, we can proceed to "Question+Answer" improvisation. However limited the range, the teacher chooses the notes to be used and teaches a Question phrase through echo-play. Then everyone answers together with an improvised phrase the same length and with the same notes. In a pentatonic scale, it sounds quite acceptable.

When most of the class is comfortable with this exercise, we can move on to individual responses to the same *tutti* Question. Going all around the class, each student answers over the teacher's drum or xylophone ostinato. Those students who are insecure may pass until they feel ready to take a turn. (This can also be reversed with solo Questions and *tutti* Answers until the children are ready to play either role.) Later, the teacher can insist that the Answer come home to whatever tonal center is chosen; and still later, that it picks up something from the Question, like a rhythmic figure or a particular melodic figure, that tells us the Answer is on the same musical subject.

When simple Question+Answer improvisation is secure, we can put two sets together, Q+A; Q'+A', over the ensemble, making clear that the four phrases now belong together and must make sense musically. A break between the sets, with only the ostinato patterns continuing, makes it much easier for the class to remember what happened and discuss it later. Which sets were most effective? Why? What carried over from the Question to the Answer? From one set to the next? What tells us that the players are "talking on the same subject"?

When this stage is reached, longer forms become possible: a Rondo, using a class Q+A set as the theme with improvised episodes; a little dance for the class to work out in small groups; a short prelude to another piece in the same key; a set of related Q+A pairs or sets, etc.

For variety, it's fun to play Pass-It-On all around the class. Each child plays one phrase over the teacher's xylophone or hand drum ostinato. (Keep the improvisation moving though any interruptions or fumbles.) Or, in small classes, set each child to improvise a melody, "follow it where it wants to go," to use Orff's phrase, and hold the last note until the next player takes over. (There need be no rules about length or tonality when the class has reached this level of proficiency.)

Like echo-play, this technique is most successful when the teacher provides a supporting "Carpet of Sound" to keep the improvisation moving. By playing across any breaks in rhythm or continuity, the accompaniment minimizes self-consciousness and enables the student soloists to relax into their assignments.

For example, when children are at the stage of using the G Pentatonic scale from D to D':

The second Question may be set through echo-play or picked up from a student's improvisation, then repeated before the second Answer by the rest of the class. Or there may be any number of original Answers by individual students. Or four volunteers may choose to do the entire sequence.

Particularly successful sets can be notated, repeated, and developed as rondo themes to recur between improvised sections. They can be used for dances or processions in dramatic play, or for transitions between large group assignments in performance. The possible creative uses of improvisation in the Orff classroom are endless.

I will not take time here to go into how Orff teachers can introduce notation, since Orff deliberately left that point open. There is no general agreement on the teaching technique to employ, except for a prior need to practice large muscle movement to secure a steady beat, in place. This is done with body percussion and carefully sequenced locomotor movement.

When introducing a new scale, I like to use scale-tune echo-play until the new sequences are familiar. Then students may improvise their own scale tunes, starting at the scale's top or bottom, and repeating any note as often as necessary (without backtracking) to make the melody come out even. Once the new scale is relatively secure, we can further improvise before shifting to printed music.

Such exercises in improvisation provide the best training in both technique and musicianship because the students are learning to *think* music for themselves. Progress may be slow at first, but as skills accelerate, it's far more rewarding for them to make their own music. Simply working through an instruction book, necessary as that can be, cannot compare or produce such joyous, musical results.

## The Role of the Recorder Repertoire

Unfortunately [in 1995], the vast number of delightful pieces for recorders and Orff Ensemble in the five volume Schulwerk and supplements are mostly available only inside these fat and expensive books. The exceptions are adapted pieces from Volumes I and II in a very small book edited by Margaret Murray, *Eighteen Pieces for descant recorder and Orff-instruments*, and in my *Carols and Anthems*, featuring pieces for recorders. Schott publishes both.

But these are just a beginning. In Schulwerk Volume I, there are only two rather demanding parts specifically for recorders. These parts obviously are to be played by the teacher, as Keetman herself must have played them originally. There are, however, many tunes among the instrumental pieces in Volume I Part III that are attractive for the recorder and of various levels of difficulty. For example, the piece in Volume I, Murray edition, page 105 is a simple tune in C Pentatonic that can be sung or played with whatever resources we choose, laid over a demanding double ostinato for Alto Glockenspiel and Alto Xylophone. It works well for soprano recorders at a relaxed tempo. On Tenor Recorder (for a child whose hands are big enough to comfortably reach) or cello, a low C would be a welcome addition – whether sustained or with a regular rhythm pattern.

The further along in the Orff-Schulwerk we go, the more recorder repertoire is available to us. This is probably because the German children of the demonstration group in the famous 1948 series of broadcasts heard in Bavarian schools, on which the Schulwerk is partially based, were new to the recorder. They had to master sufficient skills before they could play recorder pieces in the radio demonstrations.

I urge those of you who have access to the Schulwerk volumes to look through them and find for yourself some of the treasures for recorder. There are pieces with one or two accompanying bar instruments; pieces for recorder and drum; pieces for two Sopranos, Soprano and Alto, or SAT recorders, alone or over the ensemble. Personally, I find the small pieces with one or two bar instruments the most useful. The students love them, and they're always well received in performance.

Four books for recorders by Gunild Keetman, Orff's life-long collaborator, are also indispensable. All published by Schott, the first two, *Spielstücke für Blockflöten a and b*, are ideal for intermediate students who are fairly secure on soprano recorder and have recently moved on to alto and tenor. The lower voices play many ostinato patterns and some simple melodic parts. No bar instruments are scored, but there are three very exciting pieces for recorders and hand drums at the end of book *b*. These are quite sophisticated and suitable for young people and adults.

My favorites, the other two, are Keetman's books for recorder and hand drum, *Stücke für Flöte und Trommel*, Schott Ed. 3625 and 6587. Though beginning with a very simple drum part, the pieces increase in difficulty very quickly, requiring two or three different techniques. The books are chockfull of imaginative, enormously varied little pieces and challenging canons for two recorders and two drums. However, drumming techniques are not spelled out at all, so I advise getting my book, *For Hand Drums and Recorders* (Musik

Innovations), if you're interested in the technical requirements. Some of these Keetman pieces are among the most effective we've ever used in concert, and provide a welcome change from the usual consort program fare.

Let me also call your attention to Keetman's setting of Orff's text, *The Christmas Story* (Schott) in the English edition. This is for children to act out, sing, and play. It makes extensive use of recorders in consort and in various combinations with voices, strings, and Orff Ensemble.

—

*Portions of this essay were originally published in American Recorder, September 1995. Reprinted with permission.*

Addendum

Those interested in a practical approach to teaching recorder in relation to the Orff Approach may want to explore some of IMC's books listed below.

- *Recorder Improvisation and Technique*, Books One, Two, and Three, Brasstown Press
- *My Recorder Reader* Books 1, 2, and 3 and *My Recorder Primer*, Brasstown Press
- *Carols and Anthems from the Schulwerk*, Schott
- *Recorders with Orff Ensemble* 1, 2, and 3, Schott
- *For Hand Drums and Recorders*, Musik Innovations
- *Suite on Four Notes* for SR and Piano, Loux
- *A First Folk Song Suite* for 2 SR and piano, Waterloo

# 21 USING THE RECORDER: THE ORFF APPROACH

*IMC summarizes the role of the recorder in all stages of the Orff Approach, and provides a survey of the foundational Orff-Schulwerk literature, highlighting recorder music worth seeking out. In response to this article, Gunild Keetman wrote a letter to IMC, then the editor of The Orff Echo, saying it was "a special delight" to her.*

In the Orff Approach, the skilled and imaginative use of the recorder is essential from the very beginning. First, the teacher must have good command of the instrument in order to teach students to develop their playing skills. Fortunately, the recorder seems to have an immediate appeal to children, no matter how young, and lends itself to a great variety of classroom applications.

In the hands of an experienced player, the recorder is capable of remarkable musical inventiveness. It can be used in movement lessons, in listening exercises, in songs and dances with rhythmic accompaniment, in improvisation along with other Orff instruments, and as one of the chief melodic instruments within the full Orff

Ensemble. It is for these reasons, along with its ease of introduction, that the recorder is featured in the repertoire of the Schulwerk and its supplementary books.

Currently, as the Orff instruments become more widely known, more and more publications for recorders and Orff instruments are being issued. England and Germany are flooded with them – good, bad, and indifferent – and the tide is already rising in this country. It behooves us to see how this surge of recorder materials will affect our teaching choices as we become acquainted with this new repertoire.

Although these recorder pieces are by and large originally worked out for children and young people, there is no age limit on players. Year after year I have found my adult classes just as enthusiastic as my children's groups – and certainly the adults often need the rhythmic training, ensemble experience, and improvising exercises just as much.

## Essential Schulwerk Recorder Pieces

Let us consider, before anything else, the wide repertoire available for recorder in the Orff-Schulwerk. For example, in Volume I, I begin with a short and simple instrumental piece such as #8 on page 99. (Schulwerk references are to the English-language Murray edition, passim.)

A piece need not be explicitly designated for recorders to be of interest. The melody of #18, page 105, is not specifically assigned to the recorder (or to anything else) but it makes for a very interesting little piece for children with C Pentatonic scale facility. The ostinati for alto glockenspiel and alto xylophone are much more demanding than the tune itself.

The recorder is frequently employed in song settings. Sometimes it will double the tune (always an option), but more often it is the lead in introductions, interludes, and postludes. (See *Old Angus*

*McTavish*, Volume I, page 37.) This is also true of song settings in support of dances, as in *Fabian, Sebastian* in Volume II. The soprano recorder is assigned the melody over an ensemble of soprano and alto glockenspiels, alto xylophone, tympani, bass, triangle, cymbal, and bass drum.

The further you advance in Volume II, the more pieces for recorders and Orff Ensemble you will encounter. Most of them are quite musically demanding, with shifting meters and tricky articulation, such as the Volume II, page 61 piece commencing with unaccompanied recorders.

In a very different mood is the *Fools' Dance* on page 72 of Volume II, with its insistent rhythms and contrasting meters, or the famous *Bear Dance*, page 39, for soprano recorder and bass with percussion, speech and body rhythms. Another favorite is *Sereno e leggiero* in Volume II, page 90, which I have taught repeatedly to children and adults, and used in concerts with magical effect.

Volume III includes several sets of dances scored for recorders and tympani, for recorders and xylophones, for recorder choir and full Orff ensemble. There are two polkas and a set of time-change dances arranged for various recorders and a small ensemble of xylophones and bass.

Volume IV is even richer in recorder repertoire. There are several sets of little pieces for recorders alone (p. 24ff., p. 36, p. 48ff.), some others for recorders and Orff instruments, and some for a small group of accompanying instruments (p. 30, p. 128ff.) with full ensemble.

A good example is the lively dance on page 53 for two soprano and two alto recorders, glockenspiels, tambourine, hand drum, cymbals, bass drum and tympani. Or look at the delightful Dorian dance on page 68 for SS/A/T recorders, xylophones, timpani, wood blocks, tambourine, drum, and stamping. One of the most interesting is the virtuosic piece for solo recorder and hand drum (page 78) that begins with a long improvisatory phrase on the recorder before the drum enters.

There's another exciting and difficult dance (p. 84ff.) for three solo soprano recorders and choir of soprano recorders, with soprano and alto xylophones, hand drums, castanets, tambourines, cymbals and tympani. The Chaconne (p. 124ff.) is another favorite of mine in the entire Schulwerk repertoire. It begins quietly with a statement of the theme over the harmonic pattern in the alto metallophone part and then gradually builds up through the succeeding variations to a full ensemble.

Volume IV also uses recorders in a number of song settings. I particularly like the herdsman's dance at the end of the Norwegian folk song, *Gjeite Lok* (Volume IV, p. 34), the gentle Dorian *Connemara Lullaby* (p. 44), and Orff's small masterpiece *Ascension* (p. 88) for an entire choir of recorders – three sopranos, two altos, two tenors, bass – and three part choir, cymbals, and tympani.

In Volume V there are again many sets of small pieces for recorders alone, recorders and xylophones, and recorder consort with percussion and bass. There's a delightful setting of *Fum, Fum, Fum* (Volume V, p. 36), a very effective setting of the Renaissance *Midsummer Dance* on page 29, and the *Chaconne* for recorders and bass on page 61.

One of Gunild Keetman's finest instrumental pieces is the *Berceuse* for soprano recorders and Orff ensemble in the Dorian mode (p. 50ff). The melody begins over a shifting chordal pattern on D minor and G major chords in the alto xylophone. Then after a contrasting section in which the glockenspiels carry the tune, the first theme recurs with an extension into a long solo cadenza just before the coda.

It's unfortunate for recorder players that this highly varied and rewarding repertoire is so widely scattered throughout the five volumes of the Schulwerk. The only real alternative is a small collection of the easiest pieces pulled out and edited by Margaret Murray and issued under the title *Eighteen Pieces for Descant Recorders and Orff Instruments* (Schott 10917).

## Beyond the Five Volumes

Among supplementary materials in the official Schulwerk series published by Schott are two books by Gunild Keetman, *Spielstücke für Blockflöten* 1a/1b (Schott 3557-1, 3557-2). These are designed for groups in which the soprano players are already fairly accomplished and the altos and tenors have only recently transferred to the lower instruments. They are not as easy as they look, however, because of the continual demands for rhythmic tension between the parts and a great variety of articulation.

Keetman's collection of pieces composed for recorder ensemble and percussion, *Spielstücke für Blockflöten und kleines Schlagwerk* (Schott 3575), is still more demanding, requiring skilled recorder players and even more expert percussion players.

Both children and adults particularly enjoy Keetman's small book of pieces for soprano recorder and hand drum, *Stücke für Flöte und Trommel* (Schott 3625). They provide incomparable rhythmic training and are especially useful for groups without the bar instruments of the standard Orff instrumentarium – there is only one piece requiring any accompaniment beyond hand drum or tambourine. The pieces are astonishingly varied, including lively dances, pastorals, stately processionals, and a whole set of rhythmically complex and delightful canons for two recorders and two drums. We have played several in concerts and they are always among the favorites, whether the audience is adult or children.

One final title in the Schulwerk series demands attention. That is Gunild Keetman's setting of Orff's text of "The Christmas Story." Since the first performance by a cast of children on the Bavarian radio network in 1948, it has remained among the most popular and effective of the Schulwerk associated works, even if some of the humor is lost for us in Margaret Murray's sturdy British English translation, for the original text is in the very colorful Bavarian dialect of Orff's native home.

"The Christmas Story" is scored for children's choir, recorder consort (S/AA/T), Orff instruments, and unpitched percussion. In all but the *Gloria*, recorders are required. Particularly appealing are the Introduction and Pastoral for soprano, two altos, and tenor recorder (a cello is added in the Pastoral), the two carol settings, and the setting of the exquisite Latin carol, *Dormi Jesu*, for a choir of angels and recorders and xylophone.

Let me close by strongly recommending to all who feel the need for new repertoire – whether to play, teach, or perform – that you consider the purchase and study of at least the small recorder books by Keetman, as well as the recorder pieces collection by Margaret Murray, the British music teacher and longtime supporter of the Schulwerk.

—

*A version of this essay first appeared in The Orff Echo Volume 6 Issue 2 [February 1974]. Reprinted with permission from The Orff Echo, the quarterly journal published by the American Orff-Schulwerk Association.*

# 22 ON SETTING A PROGRAM'S GOALS

*In this essay, IMC generalizes from her direct experience formalizing the goals of her own kindergarten curriculum project. She makes the broader suggestion, now generally required of teachers, to list specific goals for every curriculum.*

A few months ago, my editor asked me to spell out my goals for the kindergarten program I had been asked to write. It seemed a needless exercise as I felt that my goals were already clear in the text itself.

But as I got into the assignment, I found it both challenging and rewarding to make myself plainly state what I was hoping to achieve, and to do so in terms that any classroom teacher could readily understand.

My resulting list here may be a useful stimulus to your review and clarification of your own goals in your own teaching situation.

Goals of the IMC Kindergarten Program, "Music Plus"

*To provide basic rhythmic training through movement, speech, singing, and instrumental play.*

Rhythm training will include individual movement exploration, both in place and in common locomotor movement; practice in following a common pulse through body rhythms, movement; participation in rhythmic activities in response to sound cues, instrumental accompaniment, verbal cues, rhymes poems, and/or songs; responding to sound signals; participating in set singing games in a variety of floor patterns, both as leader and follower; improvising new ways of doing familiar activities.

*To develop the musical use of speech.*

Speech Play includes training in using single sounds – long vowels, consonants, and blends – that many children find difficult; echoing exactly the words, names, rhymes they hear, using a variety of inflection, tempo, dynamics, vocal timbre; accompanying rhymes, sayings, and short poems with vocal ostinati; answering and asking questions in the context of melodic improvisation wherever their voices lie; dramatic play; moving in response to verbal cues, names, rhymes, poems; using speech patterns as rhythmic building blocks; abstracting rhythm patterns from their corresponding speech patterns to make independent rhythmic compositions.

All of these activities focus on the musical qualities of speech and the concepts that transfer to music training; allow scope for individual experimentation and leadership when the children are ready; cultivate respect for and enjoyment of the spoken language and our oral tradition.

*To develop aural memory.*

Echo-play in speech exercises, in body rhythm play, in the use of rhythm instruments, in singing within a very limited range; develop a sure sense of similarities and differences, and gradually extend the aural memory as the focus narrows to pitch perception and performance, whether singing, playing, or doing a singing game.

Use cumulative songs, response songs, narrative songs – all to build memory and concentration.

*To develop aural discrimination.*

Echo-play in speech and song, and a variety of listening games providing the basis for recognizing and differentiating the various sound sources available in the classroom: objects, body rhythms, vocal sounds, found instruments, unpitched percussion, pitched bar instruments, piano or recorder.

Movement in response to different sound sources to develop awareness of timbre, of sound quality.

Classroom instruments are introduced first as sound signals via the teacher's hands, and then used for color and punctuation in sound stories and sound settings of poems. Introduce instruments one by one for movement response; only then put them into children's hands for specific assignments such as signals, for color, as substitutes for familiar words, in developing little rhythmic compositions, and as sound and silence, pulse and pattern, solo and group independent ostinato patterns.

*To develop the singing voice.*

Improvisation is used from the very beginning; children learn to find their own voices and sing in their comfortable range. Later, tone-matching games are introduced, based on what they are able to sing. Only then are they expected to match pitches in limited range songs on *So-Mi* or *So-Mi-La*.

Folk songs have been classified into several different categories to make clear what is expected:

Limited Range songs are for everyone to sing as accurately as possible;

Response songs are for the teacher to sing and the class joins in on the clearly marked (very simple) responses;

Sing-Along songs are in a limited range that most of the class can sing spontaneously or with minimal teaching;

Activity songs are for the teacher to sing and the class to respond to as the words suggest;

Singing Games songs are for the teacher to sing and the class to play the game as traditionally done; children sing if they are able to do so;

Resting songs are for the teacher to sing to the children as they relax after active play.

*TO DEVELOP BASIC INSTRUMENTAL TECHNIQUES.*

Good technique in using the basic body-rhythm gestures provides the foundation for all later instrumental play. Unpitched percussion instruments are used sparingly and with specific aesthetic intent and correct technique from the beginning.

Patschen exercises prepare for the introduction of the xylophone and glockenspiel later. These instruments are used to support the singing voice in simple ensemble settings.

Instrumental play moves from our first instruments, our bodies, to simple percussion instruments played with the hands and fingers. Advance later to those played with mallets – a gradual externalization of the means of music making. All three stages develop large muscle movement before small muscle control is required, as with learning conventional instruments.

*TO DEVELOP VISUAL, KINESTHETIC, AURAL, AND VERBAL IMAGINATION.*

Discovered in a variety of multi-sensory experiences, particularly through the use of dramatic play.

TO DEVELOP TASTE, INDEPENDENT JUDGMENT, AND DIVERGENT THINKING.

Materials are carefully chosen. Rhymes, poems, stories, games, sayings, and songs are chosen for their own intrinsic worth, not simply for pedagogical purposes. Real choices are presented to the children, so they have to begin making their own decisions about what is, or is not, effective; about the resources to use in a particular context.

Almost all the material comes from our American folk heritage or from recognized poets and storytellers.

TO REINFORCE ACADEMIC LEARNING.

Particularly in Language Arts and the use of numbers, supported in a play context through rhythmic games.

TO MAKE THE BEST INTRODUCTION TO FORMAL MUSIC EDUCATION.

For kindergarteners, a joyous experience and a multi-sensory basis for all future learning.

—

*A version of this essay first appeared in The Orff Echo Volume 14 Issue 2 [Winter 1982]. Reprinted with permission from The Orff Echo, the quarterly journal published by the American Orff-Schulwerk Association.*

# 23 THE SCHULWERK'S ORIGINS AND EARLY MUSIC

*Toward the end of her career, IMC compiled this survey of Medieval and Renaissance music in the foundational Volumes of the Schulwerk. As she prepared notes for this article, I imagine she felt a sense of the full circle of her interests. Prior to meeting the work of Orff and Keetman, she was already a scholar of Early Music, and became a life-long performer of that repertoire in consorts and ensembles.*

After completing his undergraduate work in Munich, Carl Orff spent several years in Berlin under the aegis of Curt Sachs, the famous musicologist, who became his mentor and friend. Here Orff was immersed in early music for the first time. It was during this period that he began to explore the Medieval and Renaissance roots of European music. This experience altered his own style of composition to such an extent that he destroyed much of his earlier works.

He was particularly fascinated with the sudden development of early opera as in Monteverdi's opus and undertook a new performance edition of Monteverdi's *Orfeo*, published in 1925. Orff's own operatic works would derive from this monodic style, with the admixture of dissonance and mixed meters impossible for early 17th Century composers.

Collaborating at the Güntherschule, by then well established in Munich, Orff and his colleagues Dorothee Günther, Gunild Keetman, Maja Lex, Hans Bergese, and others prepared and published a wealth of material. These included exercises for speech play, chorus, ensemble play, and dramatic movement. Much of this published work had been stimulated by a new, increased interest in the musical possibilities of even the simplest of Medieval and Renaissance melodies and the compositional and performance techniques of those earlier times.

In 1933, *Elementare Musikübung* appeared, the first book in an eventual series of works collaboratively written by Orff and Keetman. Since it was designed for college-age students, it moves at a much faster pace than the five volumes of the Schulwerk. Right off, Part I starts with twenty pages of increasingly demanding rhythmic and melodic exercises – many are developed further in a later section. Part II begins with monodic modal tunes, but by #10 there is an added drone accompaniment, and at #29 ostinato is introduced. All of these musical exercises were intended for extension through student improvisation and movement. The book's final section has Orff's own captivating developments of a few of the barebones exercises in Part I.

Many more "small gray books" embodying the same methods became part of a first "Orff-Schulwerk" series. However, these are not all by Orff. Gunild Keetman, who would continue to be his lifelong professional partner in music education, was also prolific. Beginning with *Erstes Spiel am Xylophon* (Schott 5582), her contributions were invaluable. In that book she focuses on playing the xylophone, with drones and ostinati accompaniments for her delightful tunes that are incredibly varied and ingenious.

When the Nazis closed the Güntherschule in 1944 during World War II, it seemed all this wonderful experimental work in music education would be forever in limbo or lost. That appeared likely, had it not been for the unexpected invitation to Orff from Bavarian Radio in 1954 to "do a few programs for the schools." This off-chance opportunity led to further successful broadcasts directly fed into Austrian schools, and eventually to the reincarnation of Orff pedagogy for younger children in the Schulwerk volumes we know so well.

Reworked over the years 1950–54, the "official" Orff-Schulwerk by Orff and Keetman is based on their earlier work of the 1930s, but transmuted by the educational radio programs for school children, expanded, revised, and organized into the five-volume version published in German. The standard edition in English is, of course, Margaret Murray's, an Orff enthusiast who consulted directly with Orff and Keetman. She did not translate the entire Schulwerk verbatim, but made suitable British substitutions for heavily Germanic source materials and reset material with permission. Some of her own books draw directly upon Schulwerk pieces, or exemplify Orff principles, as in her original settings of old English folk songs, hymns, and other historical works.

Given the importance placed on traditional and pre-Classical Western music in the Schulwerk, and with our current emphasis on well-known folks songs in the Orff Approach for children, a review is in order of what Early Music materials are to be found in each of the five volumes.

## In Volume I

Because in central Europe there is no tradition of old pentatonic song, there was nothing ancient to use for this first volume. All the "folk melodies" set were more or less invented by Orff or Keetman. They were simply unaware at the time of the European legacy of pentatonic song in Scotland, Ireland, Brittany, Normandy, and northern Spain – let alone on this side of the Atlantic.

Furthermore, all of their tunes are in *Do* Pentatonic, as they were unfamiliar with other pentatonic scales. There are only occasional examples of pentatonic paraphony in accompaniments: For instance, the Soprano Xylophone in *Wee Willie Winkie* or in the vocal parts of such as Orff's *Alleluia* (page 28). There is also ingenious variety in the structure of the supporting drones. These include such significant examples as: Repeated eighth notes on the dominant in *Unk, Unk, Unk* and sustained open fifths in #28, (page 22); a repeated, low sustained tonic coupled with a higher open tonic fifth in the canon on page 32; the dominant drone throughout an entire section of *Boomfallera* until the final tonic.

## In Volume II

In Volume II there are only three settings of early melodies.

There is the 16th Century tune of *A Farmer Went Trotting* on page 54ff, set with a tonic chord or fifth in the bass and a two-bar ostinato for Soprano Xylophone in the verse and Alto Xylophone in the chorus. This is arranged first with the tune in unison, then in a four-part canon.

Far more interesting musically is the famous 13th Century English canon, *Sumer Is Icumen In* on page 80ff. with a four-part canon, persistent shifting tonic and supertonic chords, and supporting contrapuntal melodic four-bar ostinato for the other two voices.

The third example is *King Herod and the Cock* on page 92, set to an old German tune from Yugoslavia and arranged in paraphony over tonic drones or shifting chords.

## In Volume III

Since Volume III is concerned with introducing hexatonic and full major scales with dominant and subdominant chords, there are few old tunes included, and those that do appear are quite atypical of their periods. For instance, the children's game-song, *Carillon de Vendome* on page 22, has a range of only four notes, and is accompanied by repeated tonic fifths, tonic pedal in the lowest voice and Alto Metallophone, and repeated G-C patterns in the other voices and last two bars of the bass. The melody itself is doubled a sixth below the tune, so the upper voice lies very high.

The beautiful old Irish melody *Beauty's Spell*, set by Margaret Murray, is just as atypical. The tune has a persistently pentatonic flavor, despite the passing tones on C and all the parts on the dominant throughout, with the tonic suggested only at the very end. There is no leading tone at all – scarcely suggestive of functional harmony! The *Street Song*, on the other hand, is the epitome of this technique, with its persistent chordal pattern: I I IV IV I I V V I I IV IV I V I I etc.

The variations on a 16th Century lute piece by Hans Neusiedler make up an ingenious and technically demanding performance piece. Orff's *Mater et Filia* (page 94), on the other hand, is a good example of vocal paraphony over a dominant drone. It also occasionally moves to the sixth for a little spice and variety, an old technique certainly, but in this new setting amazingly effective for voices.

## In Volume IV

The Aeolian, Dorian, and Phrygian modes are introduced one by one in Volume IV. The same techniques of tonic and dominant drones, moving drones, melodic ostinato patterns, and paraphony reoccur as in the previous three volumes. *King Herod and the Cock* (page 1 ff.), for instance, is labeled Aeolian, although it's essentially a pentatonic tune with a passing B only in in the cadence. The accompaniment consists of a simple tonic drone with a moving dominant drone on Alto Xylophone, introduced during the verse. There is a suggestion of harmonic shifts to F and D minor chords when the soprano recorder repeats the tune over the sustained fifth in the bass, along with the rhythmic ostinato patterns on bells, tambourine, and bass drum. We don't know how old the melody is.

The three French folk songs on pages 26-29 are old tunes, again how old is impossible to say, except for #2, *C'Etait Anne de Bretagne,* celebrating the marriage of Anne, Duchess of Brittany, to the King of France in 1491. (There is a more elaborate setting of the same song in *Paralipomena,* another Schulwerk book, that for a more authentic sound includes recorders, sordun, treble or tenor viol, and double bass.). *J'ai vu le Loup* as well as *C'Etait Anne de Bretagne* are set with moving drones, very simply and effectively. *Marmotte* may be an old minstrel song from Savoy. As singers enter for a festive program or a Christmas Madrigal dinner, it can serve as a very effective instrumental piece for a Farandole. (I advise varying the recorder assignments as the dance goes on.) These three songs also are good for playing by a recorder trio, with the bass sustaining the low tonic drone.

One of my favorites for a good soprano vocal soloist and choir is *Amor, Amor* on page 37. Except for the Glockenspiel interlude at the end of each verse, the parts are both easy and magical with their relaxed and quiet rocking movement. It's unknown how old the melody is, only that this song was widely admired and sung over much of Europe.

Margaret Murray has given a Dorian flavor to her setting of the hexatonic 15th Century English carol, *A Babe Is Born* (page 42). She uses parallel fourths in the Alto Glockenspiel part in her unusually elaborate arrangement.

Pages 50 and 51 have a set of four *Pastorales* for recorders in three-part paraphony over a tonic drone. Two of these are derived from pieces in Orff's very first "Schulwerk" publication for Güntherschule students, as is the melody of the familiar dance on page 68.

*C'est le Mai*, a very old French pentachordal melody with alternating solo and choral sections, appears in a simple setting on page 52. Again, it derives its Dorian flavor only from the paraphonic accompaniment to the last phrase. Wandering minstrels sang it as they went from house to house in the villages and towns of Champagne and Lorraine on May Day centuries ago.

Part I of Volume IV ends with Orff's mini-masterpiece, *Ascension*, which dramatically employs the paraphonic techniques of earlier centuries. It is incredibly effective with a good choir and competent players.

Part II, labeled "Triads," has only two old melodies. The 15th Century *When Mary Through the Garden Went* on page 99 is an unusual setting with the unsupported melody alternating with parallel fourths in the Glockenspiels throughout. After the first two phrases. an underlying tonic drone is added. The early 17th Century *Three Angels Are Singing* (page 122) uses parallel triads throughout the vocal parts doubled by both Soprano Glockenspiel and Alto Glockenspiel over a multiple tonic drone in xylophones, Alto Metallophone, and bass alternating with timpani. The interlude/coda between verses introduces a new melody with shifting C and D chord patterns in the accompaniment.

Also, Volume IV introduces two other important historical techniques, with examples by Orff and Keetman. First, the "Decoration of the Third" over moving open fifths (p. 118 ff.) and secondly, the later elaboration of this technique into the Chaconne, a series of ornamented melodic improvisations over the same harmonic pattern. (See Keetman's *Andante con moto* on pages 124-127.) Note the surprisingly intense dissonance of the repeated E's on soprano or alto xylophone in the first two variations, and again, in the new, eighth-note figures in the final recorder parts section leading up to the *ff* ending. On page 130 there's another Aeolian Chaconne in 5/8 time for Soprano Recorder and Alto Xylophone plus castanets, which gives a contemporary twist with its shifting meter. It is both short and easier to put together.

I should mention there is an interesting addition to the notes in the very back of Volume IV. Here for the first time in the Schulwerk is mentioned the possibility of using minor pentatonic scales in melodic improvisation. A few incomplete examples, to be finished out by students, are included. In the examples, broken tonic triads or tonic and dominant fifths are used in alternating patterns, along with some freer ostinato patterns. These are no doubt suggestions by Keetman, who had been experimenting with these scales years earlier in her Güntherschule days and in her "little gray books" for xylophones or recorders. But it is still left to us to collect a repertoire of minor-penta-tonic folk songs from our own folk traditions and set them for our class use.


### In Volume V

The many 15th and 16th Century folk songs in Volume V appear in simple harmonic settings, often with tonic and/or dominant drones throughout the melody and a final coda with a dominant tonic cadence. The first example, *La Légende de St. Nicholas* (#5) is a grue-some tale of a butcher who murders and pickles three young children who are later miraculously restored to life by St. Nicholas. I can't imagine teaching it to children! But it's a good tune and could be used effectively with soprano recorders on the melody, perhaps later doubled at the sixth by the altos. Indeed, the tonic drone could be assigned to tenor and/or bass recorder, with guitar or autoharp chords in the coda, suitable for a Branle Double dance or, at a slower tempo, a Pavane. Both text and melody come from a 1582 French manuscript.

The *Old Midsummer Dance* (page 29) comes from a collection of 1540. The setting simply doubles the melody in Soprano Recorder and Alto Recorder above a simplified harmonic accompaniment for Tenor and Bass Recorder over the tonic fifth, except at the cadences, where the usual V-I progression occurs. (In the middle there's a VII-I cadence.)

A more typical four-part setting of the same dance appears on page 128, along with many valuable suggestions for further development in similar exercises. This tune is apt for improvisational ornamentation, no matter how simple, in the Soprano part while the Alto sustains the original tune an octave lower. Whether the original dance was a Branle Double, a Pavane, or an Allemande we don't know, but any of these slow dances would work. (For the dance steps to come out evenly, the final chord must be extended for a bar while a solo Soprano Recorder ornaments the cadence.)

Orff adapted *Marie Madeleine* (page 30), another old French legend song. It comes from a 16th Century Catalan manuscript through *Am Weynachtsabend*, a collection published in 1617. There are delightful metrical changes from the first 4/4 section alternating to 3/8 and 3/4 meter and back to duple time at the end of each verse. The setting is quite simple: tonic fifths or dominant octaves in the bass, occasionally doubled by Alto Glockenspiel, with a very occasional *pianissimo* triangle and a final V-I cadence. A second vocal part is added in the second verse. (There is a good English translation on page 130 of the Murray edition.) Following is another set of examples of Decorated Thirds (pages 33-4) scored for recorders. Probably these were by Keetman, as she did most of the writing for recorders.

Some of the remaining songs in Volume V worth your careful attention are:

- *Fum, Fum, Fum,* the familiar Catalan villancico, in a very effective setting on page 36. It once accompanied a dance after Mass on Christmas Day. (An English translation appears in my *Carols and Anthems from the Schulwerk,* Book I, page 18.)
- *Zu Maien, zu Maien* (page 40) in another effective simple harmonic I-V setting of an early dance song. The song itself is bi-tonal: in C major for the first phrase, in A minor for the second.
- *Carillon* is an accessible setting for two Glockenspiels of an old French melody that would be very successful in the dramatization of a folk or fairy tale, or played as a bridge between other numbers.
- The familiar old French carol, *Entre le boeuf et l'âne gris* (page 62), uses tonic drones in Alto Metallophone, Alto Xylophone and bass with a delightful *pianissimo* running scalewise descant on Soprano and Alto Glockenspiels. I had never before seen the final verse and was amazed it was included.

I should point out that there is an extremely important example on page 60 of improvisational descants on a tune, in this case an old Breton melody. The Chaconne on the next page provides another examples of the technique in a set of variations for recorders and bass on the harmonic pattern in the first four bars.

Finally, there are Orff's settings of St. Francis's *Hymn to the Sun* in moving triads over a tonic vocal drone (pages 68-70) and then *Jubilationes* in a more elaborate paraphonic setting for large ensemble and well-trained youth or adult choir.

After additional sections on advanced rhythmic training, speech settings, two demanding dances by Keetman for clappers, rattles, and percussion, and a series of speech settings by Orff, there is a short discourse on Recitative. We often used "And there were shepherds" (page 120) in Christmas concerts – but it requires a fine soloist to be effective.

## The Schulwerk, *Tutti*

Carl Orff learned the techniques of pedal point, simple drones, moving drones, and paraphony from his studies of early music. These appear throughout the Schulwerk, though tailored to the scope of each volume. Orff's frequent use of body percussion was probably suggested by the *"patschen und klatschen"* (slap and clap) of Bavarian folk dances. His exposure to the budding discipline of ethnomusicology acquainted him with the rhythmic ostinato suggested by African music and the melodic ostinato derived from Balinese music. Both enormously enrich the texture of the Schulwerk repertoire.

The Schulwerk melodies themselves are usually strophic, with much melodic repetition whether traditional or composed, so that all the elements that Orff and Keetman like to integrate are simple, repetitive, easily memorized, and easy to teach. It seems to me the supreme advantage of the Orff Approach, demonstrated in the Schulwerk volumes and other additions, is the concurrent use of both easy and demanding parts, regardless of whether in a setting of an old source or a newly composed piece. All students in the Orff Ensemble can join in, whatever their individual levels of skill, and everyone together can make music of incredible richness and beauty.

—

*A version of this essay first appeared in The Orff Echo Volume 32 Issue 2 [Winter 2000]. Reprinted with permission from The Orff Echo, the quarterly journal published by the American Orff-Schulwerk Association.*

# 24  THE ORFF APPROACH IN CHURCH

*The daughter of a church historian, IMC was married to a professor of church music (and choir director) for over sixty years. No surprise, then, that she knew her way around choir practice and music for worship, as well as children's music classes. Here, she recommends the Orff Approach to a readership of Protestant church musicians.*

The Orff Approach is finding an ever-widening place in the musical life of this country. Since its first introduction on this side of the Atlantic a little more than ten years ago, it has spoken to our condition and matched the educational philosophy of our current age better than anything else. More and more elementary schools, our colleges and universities training music teachers, and our churches with traditional music selections have turned to the Orff Approach.

Why? Because of the emphasis on participation rather than performance, on improvisation rather than interpretation, on ensemble playing and singing from the very beginning, and on movement that imparts rhythmic security.

For the first time in pedagogical history, there is a form of music education from the composer's point of view, with the focus on early ensemble experience as the basis for lifelong delight in music making.

All of this makes the Orff Approach tailor-made for the musical development of church choir singers and church musicians.

Unlike a lot of public school music teachers, churches are generally privileged in what they can decide to do. Their musicians and singers do not have to cope with a state-approved curriculum that may run counter to their own convictions. They are free to pursue individual imagination and competence at any age. That freedom, it seems to me, is resonant with the Orff Approach, for it can make some very special contributions to the musical life of any church.

Here are some of them:

- The Orff Approach can provide incomparable, basic music training for primary choirs and remedial training for older choirs.
- A whole new repertoire opens up for use in church services. There are a surprisingly large number of settings of sacred texts suitable for choirs in the five volumes of the Schulwerk. Composed by Carl Orff, one of the outstanding composers of our age, and Gunild Keetman, his lifelong collaborator, these are works of magical quality. Suitable for choirs of varying skill levels, the repertoire can be used both as finished anthems and as models for improvisations and arrangements.
- Better than anything else I know, the Orff Approach opens doors to fresh, immediate, unique ways of infusing improvisational music into the service. Imagine spontaneously improvised introits, responses, and semi-composed anthems that all employ a great variety of choral techniques and instruments.

- Last, and most important of all in the context of religious education, the Orff Approach is about character training and sensitivity to others that derives from ensemble music making. You cannot participate in an ensemble without learning to listen to your neighbors, to be aware of them and value their contributions to the whole. In the Orff Ensemble, everyone's important, whether playing a part that is easy or technically demanding.

I should also point out that in an Orff trained choir, children, particularly, can develop new respect for their fellows, and often for themselves as well. The child who has been inadequate at academic subjects or inferior at sports may find he or she has a really outstanding ability for improvisation or can play tricky rhythmical patterns that challenge their contemporaries. Such personal discoveries provide the kind of training in cooperation and the sort of healthy emotional release that our harried culture desperately needs.

As Erich Fromm notes, "Destructiveness is the outcome of the unlived life." The Orff Approach addresses both the body and the mind, and teaches us to work happily together. Music becomes again what it was for the ancient Greeks: the core of education, the synthesis of speech, movement, song, and instrumental play for unifying the personality as none of the other arts or disciplines can hope to do.

—

*A version of this essay first appeared in the Newsletter of the Association of Disciple Musicians (January 1975). Reprinted with permission.*

## 25  ON BEING SIMPLE-MINDED

*Decades before the "Slow Food" movement, and while enthusiasm in the US for the recently introduced Orff Approach was beginning to grow, IMC wrote this little reminder to calm down, enjoy the moment, and take it easy. Even in the classroom.*

There is no virtue in complexity.

One great contribution of the Orff approach to education – not just music education – is its emphasis on the vitality and beauty of simple material treated in a simple way. We keep coming back to the words "basic," "natural," and "elemental." These are words to use when explaining our new approach to music education: combining speech and song and movement and instrumental play. Particularly when our class periods are so short, we need to choose material simple enough to be learned easily, then developed a little at a time. Then we can keep adding, keep changing, and keep trying out new ways of doing old favorites when we come back to them.

Yet there is always a danger of being carried away by our own inventiveness. We can go too fast and overcomplicate the texture and interpretation of the material we choose to teach. I have seen it happen again and again in classrooms, in demonstrations, in workshops, in published material. It is so easy to drive something into the ground and make it difficult and joyless by insisting on our own plan, even when it isn't working. When our plans are too complex, too perfect, we leave nothing for the class to discover and contribute. Can't we plan alternatives and at least give them some real choice to make?

Of course our pupils must learn some basic vocabulary of song and movement, and some basic instrumental technique. But skill is not the goal, only the means to musical participation and creativity. The songs and pieces in the Schulwerk are models for us and our classes to emulate, to play, to change, and to use. The printed score is no longer sacrosanct, but a stimulus to our own interpretation and, so to speak, translation into our own context to fit our own situation and our own needs.

Trained musicians are notoriously impatient to reach some distant goal. And many music teachers make the same mistake, always under pressure to get THERE, wherever that may be. It's living for the future, getting ready for future performances, working toward some future level of achievement. This inevitably will mean skimping on basic training in rhythm, in singing, in instrumental technique, in ear training, in notation skills.

Instead of hurrying, we need to learn to enjoy and work within very strict limitations, for instance, by making interesting and musical two- and three-note tunes before we move on to the full pentatonic scale. We need to explore and enjoy the flavor of each scale and mode in turn. To explore the pentatonic repertoire and improvisation in depth before jumping into the familiar major and minor tonalities. In movement, we need to allow time for free, unstructured individual exploration before we impose pattern and form. And when we make our own arrangements, we need to remind ourselves that the object is not to use all the instruments at once, but to use them expressively, musically, and no more than necessary. We need to point out the essential quality of the song or dance we've chosen to set.

We keep saying that process is more important then performance. But do we teach that way? Do we leave room for contributed ideas as we go along? Or is the very creativity we pretend to foster being stifled by sticking strictly to our own preconceived goals?

Do we dare to have demonstrations where something new is allowed to grow? Where the process is truly demonstrated? Where our students do something they've never done before? Or do we play it safe? Do we do the old things the old way: performing what's in print without stopping to consider what *isn't* in print. Beyond a rote lesson, that's where we find the creative in the moment, doing what we and only our particular class can do together.

The whole point of the Orff Approach is to enjoy the process every slow step of the way. We must explore as we go, learning from our own mistakes and taking the time to encourage our students to share their discoveries and inventions. Neither that joy nor their understanding can be force-fed.

This real educational growth simply takes time.

—

*A version of this essay first appeared in The Orff Echo Volume 3 Issue 3 [June 1971]. Reprinted with permission from The Orff Echo, the quarterly journal published by the American Orff-Schulwerk Association.*

# PART 6

## CHAMPIONING MUSIC FOR CHILDREN

**c'**

High C

*Do'*

[eye level]

# CHAMPIONING MUSIC FOR CHILDREN

*Rhythm and harmony penetrate very deeply to the
inward places of the soul, and affect it most powerfully, imparting grace.*

PLATO

# 26  MY THEORY OF EDUCATION

*The year was 1942. The US had entered the war against Japan and Nazi Germany. Isabel McNeill, age 23, wrote this piece while in graduate school at the University of Chicago. Her views on the critical importance of education to society were already formed, in large part. Twenty years later, she'd be ready to meet the challenges and delights of the 1960s, when the Orff Approach came to North America.*

If education is a way of life, then the educational process ought to take us in the direction of personal growth from childhood to maturity. It should lead us toward the highest ends we know. Then the question immediately arises: Who is to determine the ends of education? At present, public education seems confused about both the values to uphold and the means of achieving them.

Curricula are determined to either satisfy college entrance requirements or provide vocational training. Education is regarded as a preparation for work, not as training in living. Boards of Education decide what subjects shall be taught and what teachers will teach them; boards of examiners tell the teachers how much must be covered in a school year. The teacher only decides how best to get his pupils through the approaching examinations.

Only a few progressive schools seem to appreciate the elementary fact that education is not simply a means to academic or industrial success. That it is, in fact, a fundamental aspect of life. This the Nazis have understood all too well. Their whole educational system has been distorted and abused for the purpose of establishing without question the degraded values that serve their ends. Their education has stopped short at the level of emotional susceptibility, exalting prejudice and falsehood into absolutes. Worse still, they teach egotism and cultivate cruelty and fear. They are no respecters of persons, but treat people as things, animals to be cajoled or terrorized as occasion demands.

We, on the other hand, have let an inert philosophy of materialism govern our educational practices for the last twenty years. New schools and new equipment have been extravagantly acquired, but teachers and administrators alike have continued uncritically in the same old ways. At best, perhaps, they have added a few more haphazard courses to the old curriculum, while subject matter, exams, and grades have preoccupied the schools to the exclusion of truer ends. As it is, our educational system honors conformity and social innocuousness, rather than individuality and social usefulness.

Yet if we are going to build a nation of free men, we must teach men to value and enjoy their freedom. Mostly the externalities of life are emphasized in our schools today. Particular information, particular skills, particular habits of work are declared valuable and necessary means to economic freedom. Complacency is comfortable but sterile. Inertia becomes the root of all evil. Emotional stability is all very well, but not without the emotional sensitivity that is much better.

It is easier to accept common emotional symbols than to compare and evaluate one's own prejudices. Acquiescence is immature and alien to growth. We must help the children in our schools to outgrow their uncritical prejudices and enthusiasms, to make them look for some objective reference behind the familiar symbols. We must teach them, too, to understand society as a cooperative group of individuals, and not as some impersonal institution in which the main concern will be to avoid criticism and only do what's expected.

Bureaucracy has afflicted the schools long enough. What we need now is a vast number of intelligent teachers with genuine respect for their pupils as persons in their own right. Teachers who will bring a genuine enthusiasm to their work and a thorough understanding of the place of their own subjects in the overall curriculum. Teachers who will embrace a new curriculum offering the kind of education we believe in.

If education is to accomplish its proper ends, the emphasis must be changed. People must be treated as persons and not as things; knowledge must be valued over information, understanding over skill, and social cooperation over social conformity. The curriculum will have to be reorganized toward these ends. Particular skills, information, and habits of work must be taught as a means to the good life.

The central problem remains the transfer of cultural values and the strengthening of healthy social attitudes and habits. We must educate all children to grasp a critical appreciation and historical understanding of their cultural heritage. We must cultivate their judgment and encourage them to think for themselves as much as possible so that they will be able to take an intelligent and active part in society in their maturity. This will involve mastery of language, familiarity with history, critical appreciation of the fine arts, cultivation of broader emotional loyalties, and better understanding of man's physical and social environment.

Informed comparisons seem to me the most direct method of cultivating a critical understanding of our heritage and our present cultural environment. In the teaching of literature I would include some elementary linguistics, such as was suggested in the morning's discussion. I would include, too, many assignments in the great books and comparative criticism of the ideas expressed in them.

I would choose the best poems and short stories and novels I know, and have my pupils analyze and evaluate them. Too many of the literature courses in the schools rely on inferior reading material to represent the development of our literature. I think it better to have an incomplete understanding of the best in our heritage than to completely grasp some simple tripe that educators have judged suitable for student consumption. In my experience, I have learned most in courses that were most challenging, in which the teacher expected the utmost; and I expect that other people have had similar classroom experiences. It is simply a mistake to talk down or to teach down to children, for they have more understanding than typically given credit for.

In the teaching of history, the remorseless succession of cause and effect should be supplemented by the careful study of great men and their important decisions and achievements. For too long, Materialism has governed our historical understanding to the exclusion of personal and moral values. Here again I would urge my pupils to go directly to original sources and judge for themselves, instead of relying entirely on some prescribed textbook. Elementary social anthropology would take the place of the introductory courses in economics and politics that are too coupled with history in our curricula. This would provide a basis for critical understanding of our own and alien cultures – an understanding that is imperative if there is to be any genuine cooperation among the united nations after this war is won.

The usual course in general science I would postpone until the junior year [of high school] and transform into an introductory survey course in which students would gain at least a superficial understanding of the physical and biological worlds about them.

Presumably the pupils would have learned to read with skill by then.

There should be room also for physical education. And for creative projects: painting, sculpting, manual training, weaving, music, or whatever. This should be according to the individual pupil's choice, pursued for two or three hours a week in regular school time.

In the elementary grades the main objective would still be to cultivate efficiency in the tools of thought – the three R's [Reading, 'Riting, 'Rithmetic]. But our wider aims should shape the manner and material of our presentation of these subjects. If we want to educate for freedom, we must begin as soon as children start school to enlarge their horizons. We must continually combat with knowledge the emotional prejudices that they unconsciously absorb from their families and friends.

The simplest way to go about this would be to have them read stories of children in foreign lands and in different situations in their own country. Teachers would read to them the great myths of our heritage and the folk tales of various peoples and periods – from the Bible, folk epics, and recent collections of folk tales. They should learn, too, to read aloud and appreciate the rhythm of good speech – and incidentally to pronounce correctly and to speak before others without self-consciousness or fear.

This sort of curriculum would itself train children in thinking and judging for themselves. With a base of knowledge, it would preclude the emotional bondage that cripples so many badly educated adults when it comes to making important decisions. Emotional freedom could be taught indirectly in the regular curriculum by substituting knowledge for the prejudices that have been uncritically assumed.

But that is only the negative aspect of the question. Active freedom can be learned only through social cooperation. Whether this is learned in the classroom, or not, depends on the teaching methods in use. If children are to be educated for freedom, we must let them assume social responsibility as soon as they are able to. We must encourage discussion and give pupils a chance to cooperate effectively in class. It requires an expert teacher to direct a discussion without letting it get out of hand; and this is what we need. It is just as wrong to leave everything up to our pupils as it is to take an authoritarian attitude that discourages questions and discussion.

With a background of social cooperation in class, students will have a better chance of valuable cooperation in extra-curricular activities. Interest groups and athletics provide the best opportunities for social contacts on the basis of common interests, the only possible basis for creative personal relations. This is what we must encourage if there is to be any genuine respect for other people beyond the mere "hands-off" dictum.

However, if we are to educate others for freedom, we must first be free ourselves – and be given a free rein by those who employ us. This cannot come all at once. But if we have our ends in view, we can at least work toward them to the best of our ability. We can tackle the obstacles as they arise without undue discouragement.

Education for freedom, then, is the process of guiding human development from infancy to a maturity of satisfactory personal adjustment and social usefulness. Respect for other persons, for others' ideas, for others' ways of life must be the basis of our own personality, if we are to live abundantly in the world of our fellow men.

We must understand before we criticize and we must criticize before we act. Intelligent action should be the end result of a good education. A combination of the method of comparison and evaluation on the basis of exact information, along with training in social cooperation, is the best means I know of accomplishing this end.

—

*This essay was previously unpublished.*

# 27 EDUCATING ALL OF THE HUMAN MIND

*Brain hemispheres, unite! You have nothing to lose but your "terrible dualism." In 1975, IMC was steadfast and true to her message. She deeply believed in the power of integrative methods like the Orff Approach to redress the errors Western civilization had imposed on human learning.*

Over the last ten years, distinguished psychologists like Abraham Maslow and Robert Ornstein have been telling us very forcibly that their research, and that of many others, points the way to a completely new style of education. Our Western cultural tradition and education developed and exploited the verbal, visual, logical, and sequential skills that belong to the left hemisphere of the human brain. We have largely neglected and minimized the abilities controlled by the right hemisphere, the spatial, musical, intuitive, and mystical elements of personality on which Eastern education and philosophy were built.

We have been educating, in effect, half the human mind and personality, and generally pretending the other half didn't exist. Or, if someone did take notice, the right mind faculties were treated like a stepchild, an unfortunate throwback to a more primitive stage of human development before we became rational animals.

The terrible dualism of our Western tradition – between body and soul, reason and unreason, thought and action, good and evil – has broken down in our times. No new unity looks to arise in its place. So we must deal with the world as it is. But it seems to me high time for us musicians and artists to lead the way to a new style of education: An educational approach that looks to unify the two sides of our minds and develop all of our human abilities.

We need to insist loud and long that the arts, and especially music, are inherently capable of engaging the entire personality as nothing else can. People with basic training in music and movement are more humane, more aware, more able to concentrate, more adept at cooperation than those who are denied these experiences in school. The musically educated know their own capacities and are more at home in the world than their contemporaries; they have found a healthy emotional outlet for a lifetime. Just as significant, musical training enhances the mental flexibility our modern age requires, while learning to improvise may pave the way for problem-solving confidence in other areas of adult life.

What more can we ask for our children than this kind of education?

Yet unless we music teachers muster our courage, time after time, to tell school administrators how vital music training is to children's mental health and how basic to a new educational synthesis, they will never change their position. Their opinion will remain that the arts are expendable, mere frills to be offered when there's money enough for extras and so easily eliminated when money is scarce.

When great psychologists are insisting that the arts are central to human development, it behooves us to listen and proclaim their findings from the rooftops. We must try to interrupt the established tradition of exploiting the music program and the children involved in it for the glory of the school. We should be working out a new curriculum for a new age, a new synthesis of human abilities that will answer the needs of the whole personality and become the essential core of a new kind of education in America. The key, as Carl Orff wrote in a profound insight, is this: "Tell me, I forget. Show me, I remember. Involve me, I understand."

That is what we hope for the future. Today, I know of no better way to teach both hemispheres of our brains than the Orff Approach. For the left brain, there are the traditional formal tools of music education; for the right brain, there's letting us make music in an immediate, aural way as naturally as anyone who has ever played well "just by ear." The Orff Approach integrates movement, speech, song, and instrumental play. It offers students an opportunity for ensemble playing where improvisation is cultivated and declares that participation is more important than performance.

This is the promise of the Orff Approach, to enrich our children's lives in ways we cannot calculate but can see reflected in their attitude, development, and joy in learning.

—

*A version of this essay first appeared in The Orff Echo Volume 7 Issue 3 [May 1975]. Reprinted with permission from The Orff Echo, the quarterly journal published by the American Orff-Schulwerk Association.*

## 28  LITTLE IS POSSIBLE WITHOUT HEALTHY ROOTS

*For all her humanistic philosophy and liberal politics, IMC showed a conservative streak when it came to honoring the founders of the Orff Approach. She delivered a version of these remarks at a conference of the AOSA Indiana chapter in 2000.*

Over my years as a now-and-then gardener, I have learned this much: Without healthy roots, no more growth is possible. Without healthy roots, it will be a measly harvest. It's the same in human development and organizations. We are here to celebrate our American roots in the birth of this, but our role as musicians and teachers reaches far beyond the Hoosier heartland. Our music has been enriched and stimulated by cultural contacts with other musical traditions and techniques from far and wide. But to date these are only the newest tendrils growing from the old rootstock of the European tradition, the one on which Orff and Keetman built the Schulwerk. They provided us models from our own European-influenced work. Willy-nilly, whether we like it or not, this became our heritage.

Nowadays, that music culture has been honored and imitated around the globe, with astonishing speed. Think of all the Western-style orchestras, opera companies, and virtuosi from China or Japan who fill our concert halls on tour – while our soloists and orchestras are off touring their countries. Not to mention the immediate embrace of popular American styles from Taipei to Johannesburg, from Warsaw to Tokyo.

The commerce of ideas never stops once contact is made. Still, in our time, new ideas arrive too fast for us to assimilate them properly. It seems to me we're racing around sampling foreign musical traditions like hors d'oeuvres – a little of this, a little of that. At the elementary school level, where most of us teach, this is inevitably inadequate for our needs. Except in rare instances, we're getting the merest smattering of what we then presume we can teach. Instead, in what little time we have in class, I think we'd be far better off resolving to teach our own rich tradition.

Medieval and simple Renaissance music with catchy rhythms and limited range tunes are delightful to children. They are increasingly accessible for upper graders in arrangements for voice and recorder. The recorders double or alternate with the voices over tonic drones, along with drums and the occasional bells or triangles. All are spatially separated to make the relationship of the parts clear and increase the resonance.

Research a few dances of the period. The Farandole, a gavotte-like line dance and the oldest surviving in our European tradition; the swaying Branle; the elegant, processional Pavane. Appropriate their accompanying dance tunes and put them in your own arrangements in your own classrooms. Seek out good historical models, plus use the fine examples in the Schulwerk: *Marmotte, J'ai vu la loup, Anne de Bretagne,* or *Amor, Amor.* (These can be found in Volume IV of Murray's edition.)

Go to a workshop of historical dance or a short course in the performance of early music. Practice your recorder skills so you can add the necessary heterophony in the octave above the top voice. Refer to Orff's *Umterzen* in Volumes IV and V and use them as a basis for working on your skills in devising "diversions" in a series of increasingly complex variations on a simple tune.

Cultivate your understanding of the link between Early Music and our folk songs and dances – particularly those in pentatonic and diatonic modes –and teach your students about the direct link between them. Then it's time enough for the familiar 19th Century tonic-dominant, major and/or minor melodies with their inevitable dominant cadences. I'm convinced we need to abide by Orff's decision: Postpone immersion in functional harmony until after children have been weaned away from *Do* and are firmly in touch with their musical roots. *Then* they're ready to look to other musical offspring of the European tradition, both in Europe and the former colonies. *Then* they can begin to comprehend and enjoy music from other traditions besides our own.

*They're in no hurry.* Let's allow students to first grow in contact with these ancient roots. They'll soon enough be open to new stimuli from abroad. I can suggest that classroom teachers consider inviting students with strong ethnic traditions in their families to share foreign festivals and demonstrate or teach a song or a dance or game or story. That will be authentic in spirit – not an inadequate substitute for real cultural exposure. The roots of music have become a worldwide heritage, and there's room for all, including the ever-fertile soil of European inspiration.

—

*This essay was previously unpublished.*

# 29 IMPARTED GRACE: THE CENTRAL ROLE OF MUSIC IN EDUCATION

*In the final essay of this book, IMC cites authorities from Lewis Carroll to Plato, but returns, as she often did, to Gunild Keetman and Carl Orff. In the end, she modestly advocates trust. Trust in the process of building lives, well beyond the walls of the music classroom.*

The role of the arts is more important every day in a world of rapid change where "facts" recede into obsolescence within a few years. People who depend on imparting facts find themselves in the unhappy position of the Red Queen in Lewis Carroll's *Through the Looking-Glass*, running as hard as she can to stay in the same place. Always under pressure to keep up and never able to relax, they try to stay abreast of the latest developments in their fields.

The old style of education in which the teacher's role was seen as filling "empty vessels" with facts (on which the recipients could depend for the rest of their lives) is no longer valid. Yet the old teaching techniques linger on. The teacher is still cast in the role of an all-knowing authority imparting knowledge to inferior beings, namely, students. The students' educational goal is to conform and, in the process, ape adult behavior as much as possible.

Most teachers nowadays rationally accept the need for change in education, but many of them find it impossible to leave old patterns behind. They are afraid of the children they teach, afraid of losing control, afraid of doing things differently and perhaps failing in the attempt. Music teachers are particularly tense about their role, tied up as they often are with the old habits of exploiting children. Yes, "exploiting," in the sense of mainly looking to glorify the school by scheduling performance after performance, whether or not it serves the children's real needs. It's never about a class sharing what they've been learning, or students demonstrating how to pull together to finish material they've been working on.

Is it any wonder that many music teachers are treating music in the schools as primarily recreation for children and public entertainment for parents, missing completely the central role that the arts play – especially music – in the education of the future. I say *especially* music, because as children have always known and as Orff has redis-covered for us, music is an inclusive art. Only music brings together speech, movement, song, and instrumental play as aptly as Plato declared long ago, for "rhythm and harmony penetrate very deeply to the inward places of the soul, and affect it most powerfully, imparting grace."

How could we teach music to affect children that way?

It seems to me there are three considerations: the climate of the class-room, the repertoire we choose to teach, and the exercises of impro-visation.

Questions for you, the teacher. The climate of your classroom, does it nourish growth? Are you comfortable with the children and are they comfortable with you? Are you going too fast? Why? To satisfy your own musical ambition or needs, or to impress others?

Do you allow your students to help one another? Do you allow the kind of repetition children need, and encourage new ways of doing old things? Do you trust your students enough to let them learn by making mistakes? Do you sometimes let them work by themselves on clearly defined projects for which they have been well prepared to succeed?

Every human being has an impulse for growth. We need not try to force it. Forced growth, being unnatural, will soon wither and fail, misleading us for a short time with its artificial hothouse blooms. Remember also that tension and pressure inhibit growth. If you are tense, you spread the contagion. The more capable students grow increasingly competitive and the less able become inert.

As teachers, we need to learn to minimize our own role, to use only as much authority as necessary. We should resist the impulse to impose our will on the class when they need to find their own way, if under our guidance. Maria Montessori certainly understood this very well. She insisted on having an environment where the teacher was there to help and supervise, not dominate. Patience is required, as well as a sense of humor. We need enough time for growth, as well as faith in ourselves, our students, and what we are trying to teach.

The second consideration is choice of repertoire. The best criterion I know is this: Is it worth remembering all your life? If not, forget it. Find something else that is worth teaching and passing on. Whether a playground rhyme or folk saying or song or story or an Orff-style arrangement, the same question should apply.

More publishers are becoming aware that the Orff Approach is here to stay, so we may expect a flood of materials that *look* like Orff – at least, to the uninitiated. These new materials will use the same instruments; use ostinati and borduns; sometimes include suggestions for movement. But many of them will have copied the form without honoring the spirit. They'll have seized on some obvious gimmicks without any real understanding of the Orff style; and it's our job to know the difference. The only way I can see to do this is to study the models that Orff and Keetman have provided us in the Schulwerk.

I am continually amazed at demonstrations and workshops where not a single piece by Orff or Keetman is used. If teachers and their students never know the original models on which to build, but are always playing inferior arrangements by lesser composers, how can these children possibly develop musical taste and discrimination?

The problem, I am convinced, is the teachers themselves. They have had such limited acquaintance with the Schulwerk; their training has been too short, often with only a very limited smattering of examples from various volumes. Many times, would-be Orff teachers never get beyond Volume I, or possibly Volume II, and have absolutely no understanding of the whole plan of the series and the marvelous repertoire in the later volumes.

Fundamentally, teacher training is the essential issue of Orff pedagogy in this country. If well-meaning teachers, poorly trained, dare to do in class what I have seen proposed and done in workshops, then it will eventually become too baldly apparent that they are quite unable to judge and select the materials that children might enjoy tackling.

Improvisation exercises are the third consideration. To my mind, this is the most important consideration of all, if we want our teaching to really affect the human development of our students. For this is how individual growth becomes manifest. No one can do improvisations for someone else. No one can improvise beyond their own ability or skill level. It is in improvisations that we really learn exactly where our students stand.

I have seen a child, so accustomed to failure that he cannot allow himself to try, gradually lose his inhibitions and learn that he's good, really good, at something for the first time in his life. I have seen a competitive child, always expecting to be the best, learn that her "dumb" classmates can excel at improvising, while she does not. I have seen a group of individualistic children from different, often-hostile backgrounds, learn to cooperate, to listen to others, and to become a cooperative group as well as a musical ensemble.

Perhaps they all learn there's more to their friends than they suspected; but still more important, they discover that there's more to themselves than they knew. They learned to listen to their inner voice, to follow invented melody where it wanted to go, to take, as it were, dictation from their subconscious. They played to fill the holes in the Carpet of Sound, making new ostinati accompaniments that were sensitive to the ensemble and to the players around them. They were caught up in music's imparted grace.

Improvisation in the broadest sense, then, is a superb basis for all education in a time of rapid change. Somehow we must show people how to trust and try new ideas, new ways of doing things. We teachers need to allow mistakes and to make use of them, to make contact with the deepest recesses of a child's mind and let unconscious powers find expression in new situations. We must not ignore and repress them. Like nothing else, improvisation unifies our concentration on the immediate task and can, over time, remedy our self-doubts or hesitations.

Even if we are a little afraid, here is an opportunity to grow without a barrage of facts, and a chance to augment our humanity in collaboration with others. It is the creative improvisation that is found at the heart of the Orff Approach: improvisation in speech, in song, in movement, in instrumental play, and not the least, in the art of teaching. Here is music made central to adaptable, confidence building, humanizing education.

Now, do we trust ourselves enough to do it?

—

*A version of this essay first appeared in The Orff Echo Volume 6 Issue 1 [November 1973]. Reprinted with permission from The Orff Echo, the quarterly journal published by the American Orff-Schulwerk Association.*

# THE PENTATONIC SCALES AND MODES

Not everything has to be in C Major (or *Do* Major). These tables illustrate the pentatonic scales and modes based on C, G, and F. The following characteristics of the pentatonic modes apply generally:

- Only *Do* and *La* Pentatonic modes have full tonic triads.
- *Re* and *So* Pentatonic have no Third.
- *Mi* Pentatonic has no Fifth. Thus, *Mi* Pentatonic requires a tonic drone, and may, like its diatonic cousin, the Phrygian Mode, use the Fourth or Sixth as the reciting tone. It may also make good use of the low Seventh, plus or minus a preceding Sixth in cadences.
- *Do* Pentatonic includes both tonic and submediant (vi) chords.
- *La* Pentatonic includes both the minor tonic and the major mediant (III).
- *Re* Pentatonic melodies require an emphasis on tonic and dominant to be convincing. Its scale permits the use of a typically modal VII - i cadence.

## In C:

## In G:

## In F:

# GLOSSARY

**Bar instruments** • General term applied to the Orff Instrumentarium of removable-bar pitched percussion played with mallets: glockenspiels (higher pitched metal bars), xylophones (resonant wooden bars), metallophones (resonant metal bars, lower pitched and with longer tone decay than glockenspiels).

**Bordun** • Simple drone accompaniment, typically using tonic and/or fifth only.

**Carpet of Sound** • The basis, created from layered, nonparallel, distinctive ostinati using using pitched percussion (bar instruments), in support of voice, recorder, and movement.

***Elementaria: First Acquaintance with Orff-Schulwerk*** • Gunild Keetman's distillation in one book of the philosophy and learning sequence for the Orff Approach.

**Faux-bourdon** • Also seen as the Anglicized "Fa-burden." A musical texture from Late Medieval and early Renaissance Europe, using triads in first inversion (Third-Fifth-Root, from low to high) in parallel motion.

**Gestalt** • (German; English) The entirety or organized whole grasped as more than the sum of its parts. For example, Gestalt psychology has an integrated, holistic view of the brain, perception, and learning.

**Güntherschule** • Founded in 1924 by Dorothee Günther and Carl Orff in Munich, Germany. It was a college-level school for experimental music and dance pedagogy. Closed by the Nazis in 1944, it was completely destroyed by Allied bombing in 1945.

**Hand Signs** • Also known as Curwen Hand Signs, these are a series of gestures indicating relative position, high to low, on a scale, as well as the degree of the scale in solfège (*Do-Re-Mi-Fa-So-La-Ti-Do*). John Curwen (1816-1880) developed the system for teaching groups how to sing. He attributed characteristics to each degree of the scale, for example, *Re*, "the rousing or hopeful tone" or *Fa,* "the desolate or awe-inspiring tone."

***Klang-Ostinato*** • Literally translated from German, it's a "Sound Ostinato." Also referred to in English as a "soundscape." This technique for arrangements in the Orff style typically floats voice and/or higher-pitched melodic instruments, in free rhythm, over a repetitive, lower-pitched, layered instrumental foundation.

**Locomotor** • With reference to child development, the term refers to the skills necessary for movement through space using the feet. E.g., skipping, sliding, walking, running, hopping, galloping, leaping, and jumping.

**Mozarteum** • In Salzburg, Austria, it was the first home of the Orff Institute, which it still sponsors. Founded in the Nineteenth Century, it became a university for the arts in 1998.

**Orff-Institut/Orff Institute** • In Salzburg, Austria, established in 1961; its building opened in 1963. Provides definitive training for teachers of Orff-Schulwerk.

**Orff-Schulwerk or Schulwerk** • Meaning "school [music] pieces," the German has become a general American term among Orff teachers and enthusiasts. It refers to the teachings and music resources conceived and created by Carl Orff and Gunild Keetman, or inspired by them. "Orff-Schulwerk" may also refer more narrowly to Orff volumes and printed publications, collectively. See "About the Schulwerk," starting on page 1, for more details.

**Organum** • From Medieval Europe, another line parallel to the melody, usually transposed by a perfect fourth or fifth.

**Ostinato (plural, Ostinati)** • A repeating rhythmic pattern., Derived from the Italian word meaning stubborn or obstinate.

**Patschen (German)** • Rhythmical knee slapping. In the Orff Approach, a body percussion instrument, along with finger snaps, claps, stamps. Has taken on common usage in English: one knee-slap is known as a "patsch"; the verb form is "to patsch" – a student "patsches."

***Paralipomena*** • Greek for "leftovers" or "left out"; title of the Schott publication (1966) added to the five volumes of *Orff-Schulwerk: Musik für Kinder*.

**Paraphony** • Parallel harmonic lines, often at intervals of thirds and sixths, above and below the melody. See*Faux-bourdon.*

**Schulwerk** • See *Orff-Schulwerk.*

**Schott Music** • Originally based in Mainz, Germany; one of the world's leading music publishers since 1770.

***Umterzen*** • ("OOM-tare-tzen") The historic melodic ornamentation technique, favored by Carl Orff, using "decorated thirds" usually over open fifths.

**The Volumes** • The numbered volumes (I–V) that comprise the foundational source for the study and practice of Orff-Schulwerk.

First published in German as Carl Orff – Gunild Keetman, *Orff-Schulwerk: Musik für Kinder*. Later in English as *Orff-Schulwerk: Music for Children, English Version adapted by Margaret Murray*.

In this book, "Volume" or "Vol" or "Vols" (plus Roman numeral) refers exclusively to a volume or volumes of *Orff-Schulwerk: Music for Children*, the Margaret Murray adaptation in English (UK). Occasionally, this is referred to as the "Murray Edition."

There are two other adaptations in English: (1) the Hall/Walter version, not cited in this book and (2) the "American Edition," three volumes based on the *Orff-Schulwerk: Musik für Kinder*, but heavily revised with American music pieces, edited by Hermann Regner of the Orff Institute.

# BIOGRAPHICAL NOTES

Carley, Isabel McNeill (1918-2011) • Canadian-American educator, author, and composer. First American honors graduate of the Orff-Institute (1964); a founder of the American Orff-Schulwerk Association (1968); first editor of *The Orff Echo* (1968-1983).

Carley, James Rea (1909-2004) • American composer. Professor of Sacred Music at Christian Theological Seminary, Indianapolis, Indiana (1953-1973).

Coulter, Dee • American neuroscience educator, author of *Original Mind*, 2014.

Fromm, Erich (1900-1980) • German social psychologist and psycho-analyst who viewed humanity's fundamental choice as between creativity and destructive violence.

Jacques-Dalcroze, Émile (1865-1950) • Swiss composer and educator. Influenced the pedagogy of Carl Orff. Observing piano students, he came to believe that the musicians themselves, not the pianos, were the real instruments.

Keetman, Gunild (1904-1990) • German dancer, musician, composer, and educator. Co-created the Orff Approach to music education.

Kodály, Zoltán (1882-1967) • Hungarian composer and ethnomusicologist, renowned internationally as the founder of the Kodály Method of music instruction.

Hunt, J. McVicker (1906-1991) • American educational psychologist who studied the positive effects on neglected infants of speech play with their adult caregivers.

Maslow, Abraham (1908-1970) • American humanistic psychologist who developed the Hierarchy of Needs, with self-actualization situated at the top.

Montessori, Maria (1870-1952) • Italian physician and founder of the influential philosophy of Montessori childhood education, in which instructors encourage the child's innate abilities.

Murray, Margaret (1921-2015) • English educator, musician, and composer. Translated and adapted the Schulwerk Volumes into English. Also founded the Orff Society UK. Her volumes, published by Schott from 1959 to 1965, included many English and Scottish rhymes, sayings, and folk songs. These are still widely used in Canada and the United States in Orff teacher training courses and classrooms.

Orff, Carl (1895-1982) • German composer and co-founder with Gunild Keetman, his former student, of the Orff Approach to music education.

Ornstein, Robert (1942-2018) • American psychologist and author of *The Psychology of Consciousness* (1972) and *The Right Mind* (1997).

Piaget, Jean (1896-1980) • Swiss psychologist and philosopher known for his developmental studies of children. He strongly favored a more child-centered approach to education, and greatly influenced both European and American educators.

Sachs, Curt (1881-1959) • German-American musicologist driven from Germany by the Nazis. He was a leading founder of modern organology, the study and classification of musical instruments. Likely suggested that Orff include recorders in the ensemble at the Güntherschule.

Steiner, Rudolf (1861-1925) • Austrian philosopher, architect, and educational reformer. Developed Eurhythmy and the Waldorf School educational approach.

Weikart, Phyllis S. (1931-2016) • American educator, author, choreographer, folk-dance anthologist, and researcher in kinesiology, movement, and dance. Has extensively published her research on the significance to future development of a child's ability to identify and keep a steady beat.

# RESOURCES AND REFERENCES

*From various manuscript sources in IMC's files, these are recommended resources, categorized by the editors, and annotated by IMC, for more information, insight, and repertoire ideas. Some publications are out of print, and may be available through online search.*

## Orff-Schulwerk Instructional Resources

**Keetman**, Gunild – *Elementaria: First Acquaintance with Orff-Schulwerk*, Schott.
*Excellent and indispensable. A wonderful book, organized sequentially in every area: speech play, ensemble, and movement. With innumerable fine examples for immediate use, plus full explanations of teaching procedures.*

**Orff**, Carl and **Keetman**, Gunild – *Orff-Schulwerk* Volumes I-V and supplements.

**Keetman** and **Orff**, *Music for Children (American Edition)*, Ed. Hermann Regner Books I (SMC 12), II (SMC 6), III (SMC 8). Schott.
*Essential American repertoire for beginner to most advanced Orff classes. Arranged by many leaders in the Orff movement in this country. A generous source of folk repertoire.*

**Warner**, Brigitte – *Orff-Schulwerk: Applications for the Classroom*, Prentice Hall.
*This book is basic to the intelligent development of an Orff program, spelling out in succinct detail the whole process, including Basic Rhythmic Concepts, their development in O-S, Beginning Melody and Accompaniment, Completing the Pentatonic, Forms of Accompaniment , Repertoire in O-S., Pentatonic Modes, Recorder Playing, Word and Language in O-S, and a generous sampling of her own arrangements in the Appendix. Excellent explanations, sequence, and numerous examples of appropriate American repertoire for classroom use. Detailed, practical, and immediately helpful.*

**Murray**, Margaret, Ed. – *Orff-Schulwerk Music for Children*, English Edition, Volumes I (4865), II (4866), III (4867), IV (4868), V (10920), Schott
*Essential resources for Orff teachers. Basic repertoire and techniques. Vol. I includes Speech Play, Body Percussion repertoire, plus songs and instrumental pieces.*

**Carley**, Isabel, Ed. – *Orff Re-Echoes* Book I and II, American Orff-Schulwerk Association.

## Children's Rhymes, Songs, etc. for Speech Play

**Baring-Gould**, William and Cecil, Ed. – *The Annotated Mother Goose*, Random House/Bramhall House.
*A rich source for familiar and less common rhymes, with historical notes and references.*

**Seeger**, Ruth Crawford, Ed. –
*American Folk Songs for Children*, Oak Publications.
*Animal Folk Songs for Children*, Linnet Books.
*American Folk Songs for Christmas*, Linnet Books.

**Fowke**, Edith, Ed. – *Sally Go Round the Sun: 300 Songs, Rhymes and Games of Canadian Children*, Doubleday.

**Prelutsky**, Jack, Ed. – *The Random House Book of Poetry for Children*, Random House.
*A rich and varied collection from nonsense rhymes to magical poems.*

**Ireson**, Barbara, Ed. –
*The Young Puffin Book of Verse*, Penguin Books.
*The Faber Book of Nursery Rhymes*, Hal Leonard.
*More rhymes and more varied selection than its competitors.*

**Lang**, Andrew, Ed. – *The Nursery Rhyme Book*, Dover.
*My favorite collection; fine selection plus good notes.*
(Free e-book – http://www.gutenberg.org/files/26197/26197-h/26197-h.htm)

**Sutherland**, Zena, Ed. – *The Arbuthnot Anthology of Children's Literature*, Scott, Foresman.
*An incredibly rich and inclusive collection of rhymes, poems, folk tales and stories. Full of treasures. For children of all ages.*

**De Regniers**, Beatrice Schenk, Ed. – *Poems Children Will Sit Still For: A Selection for the Primary Grades*, Citation Press.

**Livingston**, Myra Cohn – *Wide Awake: And Other Poems*, Harcourt Brace.
*Short poems for very young children. Look for her other collections, too.*

**McGovern**, Ann, Ed. – *Arrow Book of Poetry*, Scholastic.
*A delightful, imaginative selection of short poems by a great variety of poets, both American and British.*

**McCord**, David – *One At A Time, His Collected Poems for the Young*, Little, Brown.

*Lots of fine poems for children, with funny ones that would delight middle grade children.*

**Pellowski**, Anne – *The Story Vine*, Collier/Alladin.
*A stimulating collection of stories from all over the world: string stories, picture-drawing stories, stories with musical instruments, etc.*

## Recorder Instruction

**Salkeld**, Robert – *Play the Recorder*, Alfred/Chappell

**Goodyear**, Stephen – *The New Recorder Tutor*, Mills

**Katz**, Erich – *Recorder Playing: A New and Comprehensive Method*, Carl Van Roy *(S/A; good for adults)*

**Duschesnes**, Mario – *Method for the Recorder*, Parts I and II, for S or A, (Adults)

## Recorder Repertoire

**Krainis**, Bernard – *The Recorder Song Book*, Galaxy

**Mirsky**, Reba Paeff, Ed. – *House Music for Three Recorders*, Hargail
*Easy trios*

**Kulbach**, Johanna, Ed. – *Tunes for Children*, Peripole
*Good duets*

**Duschesnes**, Mario – *Easy Duets for Soprano and Alto Recorders*, Berandol Music.
*S/A Excellent arrangements*

**Keetman**, Gunild – *Pieces for Flute and Drum*, Schott
*Excellent*

**Wheeler**, Lawrence – *The Ensemble Recorder Book*, Consort Music
*Easy duets with Orff instruments*

**Rooda**, G – *95 Dexterity Exercises and Dances for Recorders*, Hargail
*Editions for either S or A*

**Carley**, Isabel – *Recorder Improvisation and Technique*, Books One, Two, Three, Brasstown Press

## Orff Repertoire

**Orff**, Carl and **Keetman**, Gunild – *Music for Children*, Books I-V, Murray edition, Schott

**Hall**, Doreen, Ed. – *Nursery Rhymes and Songs*, Schott 5143

**Murray**, Margaret, Ed. – *Wee Willie Winkie*, Schott 10916

**Keetman**, Gunild, Ed. – Chansons Enfantines, Schott 4890

**Willert-Orff**, Gertrud – *Sayings, Riddles, Auguries, Charms: Studies for Speech*, Schott 6374

**Carley**, Isabel, Ed. – *Carols and Anthems from the Schulwerk*, Books I and II, Schott 6584 and 6591

**Brocklehurst**, Brian, Ed. – *Pentatonic Song Book*, (Piano + Voice), Schott, London 11344

**Carley**, Isabel –
*My Song Primer*, Brasstown Press
*My Recorder Primer*, Brasstown Press
*My Recorder Reader 1*, Brasstown Press
*Simple Settings*, Books I and II, Magnamusic-Baton - American rhymes and songs
*Three Carols with Orff instruments*, Concordia
"Sing For The Joy Of Easter", reviewed in The Orff Echo by Marcia Lunz *Sing for the Joy of Easter*, Vol. 6, No. 1 (Nov 1973), p. 8;
"Gentle Mary Laid Her Child" reviewed in The Orff Echo by Janet Dielen, Marcia Lunz *Gentle Mary Laid Her Child*, (arranged by IMC), Vol. 6, No. 1 (Nov 1973), p. 8;
"Flemish Dance Carol" reviewed in The Orff Echo by Virginia N. Ebinger, *Flemish Dance Carol*, Vol. 21, No. 1 (Fall 1988), p. 40.

**Keetman**, Gunild – *Spielbuch für Xylophon Books* 1a and 1b
*Originally published in 1965-66, long after the five volumes of the Schulwerk.*

**Nichols**, Elizabeth – *Orff Instrument Source Book* I and II, Alfred

**Walker**, David, Ed. – Carols with Orff instruments, Concordia

**Ramseth**, Betty Ann –
*Open Thou My Lips: 12 Sacred Canons for Children*, Augsburg

*Come Sing and Ring: Christmas Songs for Children's Voices With Melody/Percussion Instruments (Orff Style)*, Augsburg Fortress
*That I May Speak: Rhythmic Speech Ensembles*, Augsburg

**Richards**, Mary Helen, Ed. – Pentatonic Songs for Young Children, Fearon

**Wuytack**, Jos, Ed. – *Musica Viva*, Leduc, Paris

**Shanet**, Howard – Learn To Read Music, Touchstone

## Ensemble Resources in the Schulwerk Murray Edition, Volume I

Body percussion, per se: pages 76ff
*Transfer to Rhythm Instruments + Speech Play using rhymes and/or sayings*
Unpitched percussion: e.g. pages 60-71
*Transfer rhythm pieces to Rhythm Instruments*
Rhythm Canons: pages 74ff
Songs with bar instruments: Vol I Part I
Preparation for Ostinato Accompaniments, pages 76ff
Ostinato Patterns: pages 82ff
Instrumental Pieces: pages 94ff

# BRASSTOWN PRESS PUBLICATIONS

*Visit BrasstownPress.com to view the entire catalogue.*

In 2011, Brasstown Press reissued Isabel McNeill Carley's best-known instructional series, *Recorder Improvisation and Technique Books One, Two, and Three*. Also published that year was *Making It Up As You Go*, a book of her selected essays.

Two years later, new editions were made available of her "Five Little Books" for beginning singers and recorder players: *My Song Primer, My Recorder Primer*, and *My Recorder Reader Books 1, 2, and 3*.

Introduced as an ebook in 2014 (and the paperback edition in 2025), this book, *Taking the Orff Approach to Heart*, is a posthumous collection of essays, some reprinted, some never published before, edited for greater accessibility by the non-specialist reader, with helpful background orientation about Carl Off, the Orff-Schulwerk, and the pentatonic scale.

Consult the full Brasstown Press catalogue, below and at brasstownpress.com, for additional information on available new and reissued books by IMC.

# Brasstown Press Editions

*Isabel McNeill Carley Orff Essentials Collection*

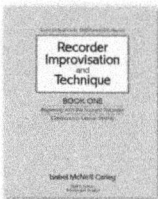

| | | | |
|---|---|---|---|
| Recorder Improvisation and Technique — BOOK ONE | Recorder Improvisation and Technique — BOOK TWO | Recorder Improvisation and Technique — BOOK THREE | Making It Up As You Go — SELECTED ESSAYS |

Eleven lessons for beginners and their teachers that explore C, G, and F Pentatonic and related modes on the soprano recorder. 46 songs and introductory exercises.
wire-o ISBN 978-1-931922-46-3
paperback ISBN 978-0-9836545-0-6

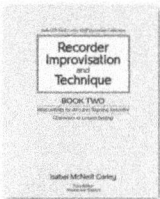

Building on RIT One, RIT Two transfers soprano fingering patterns to the alto recorder and introduces hexatonic and diatonic major and minor modes. 52 songs and intermediate exercises.
wire-o ISBN 978-1-931922-07-4
paperback ISBN 978-0-9836545-1-3

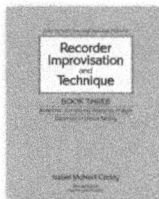

For the student already proficient on both C and F recorders. These lessons parallel the material in the Orff Schulwerk (volumes III and V). 46 challenging songs for advanced students.
wire-o ISBN 978-1-931922-08-1
paperback ISBN 978-0-9836545-2-0

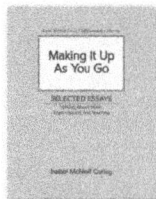

IM Carley's written work from over thirty years. The essays are grouped in three sections: Origins, Practicum, and Exhortations. Includes biographical sketch and list of IMC's publications.
ISBN 978-0-9836545-3-7

## *IMC's Five Little Books*

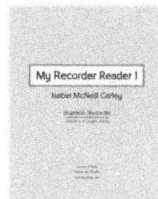

| | | |
|---|---|---|
| My Recorder Reader 1 — Isabel McNeill Carley | My Recorder Reader 2 — Isabel McNeill Carley | My Recorder Reader 3 — Isabel McNeill Carley |

The three My Recorder Reader books are a coordinated series of songs to bring a student from elementary playing to a more experienced level. Notes are added one by one to extend the student's range, with minimal instructional comments. The carefully graduated sequence of the pieces facilitates individual mastery and skill development.

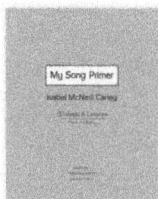

41 Songs in G Pentatonic Scale and Modes.
ISBN 978-0-9836545-6-8

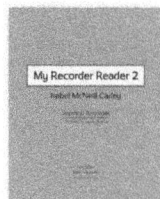

47 Songs in C Pentatonic and F Pentatonic.
ISBN 978-0-9836545-7-5

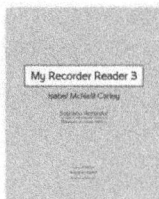

44 Songs. Expanded ranges. Pentatonic to Diatonic.
ISBN 978-0-9836545-8-2

### *Ebook & Paperback*

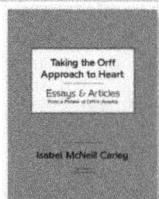

| | | |
|---|---|---|
| My Song Primer — Isabel McNeill Carley | My Recorder Primer — Isabel McNeill Carley | Taking the Orff Approach to Heart — Essays & Articles — Isabel McNeill Carley |

Establish a secure musical foundation with the step-by-step lessons offered in My Song Primer (for singing) and My Recorder Primer (for soprano recorder). Songs are interwoven in lessons with speech and rhythm exercises, suggestions for percussion and Orff instruments, and ideas for games and movement.

13 Songs, one per lesson, from So-Mi to Pentatonic.
ISBN 978-0-9836545-4-4

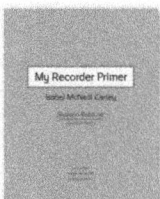

35 Songs in 6 Lessons, D-E-G-A range.
ISBN 978-0-9836545-5-1

All new essays and articles plus a read-aloud story.
ebook ISBN 978-0-9836545-9-9
paperback ISBN 978-1-931922-09-8

Brasstown Press *o* brasstownpress@gmail.com *o* brasstownpress.com

# IMC SELECTED
# BIBLIOGRAPHY

# IMC Selected Bibliography

*COMPOSITIONS, INSTRUCTIONAL WORKS, and EDITIONS*

| Year | Title | Publisher | Instrumentation |
|------|-------|-----------|-----------------|
| 1962 | Eleven Miniatures • Early Piano Recital Pieces | Galaxy; Brasstown Press | Piano |
| 1963 | Fox and Geese | Summy-Birchard | Solo beginning piano |
| 1966; 1994 | The Magic Circle: 81 Activity Songs and Singing Games for Young Children | J. Fischer; Waterloo | Singing and Activity Games |
| 1968; 1990 | Holiday | J. Fischer; Brasstown Press | Beginning piano piece |
| 1969 | A Song Primer (Updated edition 2013, renamed My Song Primer) | Brasstown Press | Voice, Body Percussion, Orff Instruments |
| 1970 | Recorder Improvisation and Technique Book One (Updated edition 2011) | Brasstown Press | Voice, Recorders, Orff Instruments, percussion |
| 1972 | Simple Settings – American Folk Songs and Rhymes with Orff Ensemble Book 1 (CDEGA Pentatonic) | Brasstown Press | Voice, Orff Instruments, percussion |
| 1972 | Carols and Anthems from the Schulwerk I (Editor) | Schott | Voice, Recorders, Orff Instruments, percussion |
| 1972 | Carols and Anthems from the Schulwerk II (Editor) | Schott | Voice, Recorders, Orff Instruments, percussion |

| 1972 | Sing for the Joy of Easter | Concordia | SSA with optional bass |
|------|---------------------------|-----------|------------------------|
| 1973 | Carols with Instruments (arr. IMC) | Concordia | Choir with Orff ensemble |
| 1973 | Flemish Dance Carol (arr. IMC) | Concordia | Unison choir w Orff ensemble and optional sopranino recorder |
| 1974 | Simple Settings – American Folk Songs and Rhymes with Orff Ensemble Book 2 | Magnamusic / MMB | Voice, Orff Instruments, percussion |
| 1974; 2001 | Recorders Plus – Original Pieces for Recorders and Orff Instruments | Brasstown Press | Recorders, Orff Instruments, percussion |
| 1975 | Recorder Improvisation and Technique Book Two (Updated edition 2011) | Brasstown Press | Voice, Recorders, Orff Instruments, percussion |
| 1976/ 1990 | More Love (Shaker, arr. IMC) | Augsburg Publishing House | Treble voices w Orff instruments |
| 1976 | Recorder Improvisation and Technique Book Three (Updated edition 2011) | Brasstown Press | Voice, Recorders, Orff Instruments, percussion |
| 1977 | On This Thy Holy Day | Augsburg Publishing House | Unison voices with Orff instruments |
| 1977 | Music for Children Orff Schulwerk American Edition Book 2 (Contributor) | Schott | |
| 1978 | My Recorder Reader 1 (Updated edition 2013) | Brasstown Press | Soprano Recorder, Voice, Orff Instruments, percussion |

| 1979 | My Recorder Primer (Updated edition 2013) | Brasstown Press | Soprano Recorder, Voice, Orff Instruments, percussion |
|------|------|------|------|
| 1979 | My Recorder Reader 2 (Updated edition 2013) | Brasstown Press | Soprano Recorder, Voice, Orff Instruments, percussion |
| 1979 | Theory Papers for C Recorders | Brasstown Press | Soprano Recorder |
| 1979 | Berceuse for Alto Recorder Solo and Alto Xylophone | Brasstown Press | Alto Recorder and Alto Xylophone or Guitar |
| 1979 | Simple Gifts (Shaker, arr. IMC) | Augsburg Publishing House | Unison treble voices with Orff Instruments |
| 1979 | Life Up Your Eyes | Augsburg Publishing House | SSA Choir and Orff Instruments |
| 1980 | My Recorder Reader 3 (Updated edition 2013) | Brasstown Press | Soprano Recorder, Voice, Orff Instruments, percussion |
| 1980 | Music for Children Orff Schulwerk American Edition Book 3 (Contributor) | Schott | |
| 1981 | The Night Before Christmas (arr. IMC) | Helicon / European American Music | Speech Choir and Orff Instruments |
| 1981 | That First Christmas Day (Stanzas by IMC; Chorus from Louise Larkin Bradford's Sing It Yourself; arr. IMC) | Choristers Guild | Two-part voices with Orff Instruments and Violoncello or Guitar |

| | | | |
|---|---|---|---|
| 1982 | Recorders with Orff Ensemble I | Schott | Recorders, Orff Instruments |
| 1982 | Music for Children Orff Schulwerk American Edition Book 1 (Contributor) | Schott | |
| 1982 | Amazing Grace (arr. IMC) | Augsburg Publishing House | Two-part voices, Soprano Recorder, Orff Instruments, Violoncello |
| 1983 | For Hand Drums and Recorders | Musik Innovations | Recorders, Hand drums and percussion |
| 1984 | Theory Papers for F Recorders | Brasstown Press | Alto Recorder |
| 1984 | Recorders with Orff Ensemble II | Schott | Recorders, Orff Instruments |
| 1984 | Recorders with Orff Ensemble III | Schott | Recorders, Orff Instruments |
| 1984 | Festive Peal | Augsburg Publishing House | Choir and Orff Instruments |
| 1985 | Recorder Improvisation and Technique (Chinese / Taiwan edition) | Brasstown Press | Soprano Recorder and Orff Ensemble |
| 1986 | Shepherds, Rejoice (Shapenote, arr. IMC) | Choristers Guild | SA Voices with Orff Ensemble |
| 1986 | Wasn't That A Mighty Day? (arr. IMC) | Augsburg Publishing House | 3-part Treble Choir with Orff ensemble |
| 1986/ 1993 | Summer Suite – Allegretto, Andante Cantabile, Circle Dance | Joseph A Loux | SAT Recorders and Percussion |

| Year | Title | Publisher | Instrumentation |
|---|---|---|---|
| 1988 | The Christmas Star (Folk Carol, arr. IMC) | Choristers Guild | Unison voices w keyboard, Orff instruments |
| 1989 | Suite on Four Notes | Joseph A Loux | S/T Recorder with Keyboard or Continuo . |
| 1990 | A First Folk Song Suite – Old Joe Clarke; Hot Cross Buns Theme and Variations; When the Train Comes Along; Oats, Peas, Beans Jig | Waterloo Music / Brasstown Press | SR SR and piano |
| 1990 | Sing We Noel / On Christmas Night | Augsburg Fortress | 2-part Treble Choir with Orff ensemble and optional 2 recorders |
| 1990 | Suite in C – Intrada, By the River, Badinerie, Gigue | Brasstown Press | Alto Recorder and Piano |
| 1991 | Mountain Carol | Choristers Guild | Choir with Orff ensemble |
| 1991 | Picardy (arr. IMC) and Star Song | Augsburg Fortress | Handbells 2 octaves |
| 1995 | Carley Recorder Series: Á La Claire Fontaine – Theme with Six Variations; | Waterloo | Soprano Recorder and Piano |
| 1995 | Carley Recorder Series: Silly Suite – Songs from Nova Scotia: Paddy Backwards, Old King Coul, The Quaker's Courtship, The Crocodile (arr. IMC) | Waterloo | Soprano Recorder and Piano |
| 1995 | Carley Recorder Series: Suite Québecoise – Ah, Si Mon Moine Voulait Danser; The Huron Carol; A Saint Malo; En | Waterloo | Soprano Recorder and Piano |

Roulant, Ma Boule Roulant
(arr. IMC)

| | | | |
|---|---|---|---|
| 1995 | Carley Recorder Series: Simple Suite – March, Scherzo, Quiet Song, Dance Rondo | Waterloo | Soprano Recorder and Piano |
| 1995 | Carley Recorder Series: C'est La Belle Françoise – Theme with Five Variations | Waterloo | Soprano Recorder and Piano |
| 2000 | Renaissance Dances for Dancers Young and Old (with CD) | Warner Bros. Publications | Piano, Recorder and Orff Ensemble, Dancers |
| 2000 | Medieval and Renaissance Dances for Recorders, Dancers and Hand Drums | Memphis Musicraft Publications | Recorders, Hand Drums, Dancers |
| 2011 | Recorder Improvisation and Technique Book One Fourth Edition – Beginning with the Soprano Recorder | Brasstown Press | Recorders, Orff Ensemble |
| 2011 | Recorder Improvisation and Technique Book Two Third Edition – Intermediate for Alto and Soprano Recorder | Brasstown Press | Recorders, Orff Ensemble |
| 2011 | Recorder Improvisation and Technique Book Three Second Edition – Advanced – Composing, Arranging, Analysis | Brasstown Press | Recorders, Orff Ensemble |
| 2013 | My Song Primer Third Edition • 13 Songs & Lessons from So-Mi to Pentatonic | Brasstown Press | Voices, Percussion and Orff instruments |
| 2013 | My Recorder Primer Third Edition • 35 Songs in 6 Lessons, D-E-G-A | Brasstown Press | Soprano Recorder and Orff instruments |

| | | | |
|---|---|---|---|
| 2013 | My Recorder Reader 1 Fourth Edition • 41 Songs in G Pentatonic | Brasstown Press | Soprano Recorder and Orff instruments |
| 2013 | My Recorder Reader 2 Fourth Edition • 47 Songs in C and F Pentatonics | Brasstown Press | Soprano Recorder and Orff instruments |
| 2013 | My Recorder Reader 3 Fourth Edition • 44 Songs from Pentatonic to Diatonic | Brasstown Press | Soprano Recorder and Orff instruments |

## VIDEO

| | | | |
|---|---|---|---|
| 1990 | Video: Speech Play – The Magic of Words (1 hr 21 min) | American Orff-Schulwerk Association | AOSA National Conference, Denver, CO November 1990 |
| 1990 | Video: Speech Play – from Speech to Song (1 hr 8 min) | American Orff-Schulwerk Association | AOSA National Conference, Denver, CO November 1990 |
| 1990 | Video: Speech Play – Storytelling Plus (1 hr 30 min) | American Orff-Schulwerk Association | AOSA National Conference, Denver, CO November 1990 |

## RECORDED MUSIC

| | | | |
|---|---|---|---|
| 2000 | Music CD: The Carley Consort • Volume I – Christmas | Chenille Records | Live recordings, 1968, 1969, 1972 |
| 2001 | Music CD: The Carley Consort • Volume II – In Performance | Chenille Records | Live recordings, 1969, 1972 |

## ARTICLES and EDITIONS

| | | | |
|---|---|---|---|
| 1969 | Editorial (The Atmosphere in the Classroom), The Orff Echo Vol 1 No 2 | American Orff-Schulwerk Association | |
| 1969 | Editorial (Music with a Difference), The Orff Echo Vol 1 No 3 | American Orff-Schulwerk Association | |

| | | |
|---|---|---|
| 1969 | Supplementary Instruments I: Strings, The Orff Echo Vol 1 No 3 | American Orff-Schulwerk Association |
| 1969 | Editorial (On Creativity), The Orff Echo Vol 2 No 1 (published as Vol 1 No 4) | American Orff-Schulwerk Association |
| 1971 | On Being Simple-Minded, The Orff Echo Vol 3 No 3 | American Orff-Schulwerk Association |
| 1973 | Editorial (The Central Role of Music in Education, The Orff Echo Vol 6 No 1 | American Orff-Schulwerk Association |
| 1974 | The Use of the Recorder in the Orff Approach, The Orff Echo Vol 6 No 2 | American Orff-Schulwerk Association |
| 1975 | The Use of Improvisation in Recorder Teaching, The Orff Echo Vol 7 No 2 | American Orff-Schulwerk Association |
| 1975 | Orff Is the Answer, The Orff Echo Vol 7 No 3 | American Orff-Schulwerk Association |
| 1975 | Orff in Church, Association of Disciple Musicians Newsletter (reprinted in The Orff Echo Vol 8 No 2) | Association of Disciple Musicians |
| 1975 | That Lovely Two-Headed Betsy Higginbottam, The Orff Echo Vol 8 No 1 | American Orff-Schulwerk Association |
| 1977 | The Next Ten Years, The Orff Echo Vol 9 No 3 | American Orff-Schulwerk Association |
| 1977 | Orff Re-Echoes Book I, (Editor) | American Orff-Schulwerk Association |

| 1978 | Concerning Rabbits, The Orff Echo Vol 10 No 3 | American Orff-Schulwerk Association |
| 1978 | About Improvisation, Music for Children Orff-Schulwerk American Edition Book 3 (reprinted in The Orff Echo Vol 11 No 1) | Schott Music Corp |
| 1978 | Gunild Keetman: Reminiscences of the Guntherschule (Translator, with Rosemarie Kelischek) | American Orff Schulwerk Association |
| 1981 | Ersatz Orff, The Orff Echo Vol 13 No 4 | American Orff-Schulwerk Association |
| 1982 | On Teaching Styles, The Orff Echo Vol 14 No 4 | American Orff-Schulwerk Association |
| 1982 | Setting Goals, The Orff Echo Vol 14 No 2 | American Orff-Schulwerk Association |
| 1982 | On Models, The Orff Echo Vol 15 No 1 | American Orff-Schulwerk Association |
| 1983 | On Patterns, The Orff Echo Vol 15 No 3 | American Orff-Schulwerk Association |
| 1983 | Once Is Never Enough, The Orff Echo Vol 15 No 4 | American Orff-Schulwerk Association |
| 1983 | The Realm of the Pentatonic, The Orff Echo Vol 15 No 4 | American Orff-Schulwerk Association |

| 1983 | Where Do We Begin, The Orff Echo Vol 15 No 2 | American Orff-Schulwerk Association |
|------|---------------------------------------------|-------------------------------------|
| 1984 | Interview with Barbara Haselbach (with Jacobeth Postl), The Orff Echo Vol 16 No 4 | American Orff-Schulwerk Association |
| 1985 | Orff Re-Echoes Book II, (Editor) | American Orff-Schulwerk Association |
| 1986 | Orff-Schulwerk in Taiwan: A Personal Report, The Orff Echo Vol 18 No 2 | American Orff-Schulwerk Association |
| 1988 | On Magic, The Orff Echo Vol 21 No 1 | American Orff-Schulwerk Association |
| 1990 | On Transformations, The Orff Echo Vol 22 No 4 | American Orff-Schulwerk Association |
| 1991 | Tips to Recorder Teachers, The Orff Echo Vol 24 No 1 and Vol 24 No 2 | American Orff-Schulwerk Association |
| 1992 | The Magic Carpet, The Orff Echo Vol 24 No 4 | American Orff-Schulwerk Association |
| 1994 | Hand Drums – Techniques and Repertoire, Orff Canada Ostinato Vol 20 No 2 | Orff Canada |
| 1994 | The Ostinato in the Classroom: Classic Examples, The Orff Echo Vol 27 No 1 | American Orff-Schulwerk Association |
| 1995 | The Role of the Recorder in the Orff Approach, American Recorder Magazine, Sep. 1995 | American Recorder Society |

| | | |
|---|---|---|
| 2000 | Early Music in the Schulwerk, The Orff Echo Vol 32 No 2 | American Orff-Schulwerk Association |
| 2001 | Playing with Our Materials: Speech Play, The Orff Echo Vol 34 No 1 | American Orff-Schulwerk Association |
| 2011 | Making It Up As You Go • Selected Essays – Writing about Music, Improvisation and Teaching | Brasstown Press |
| 2014 | Taking the Orff Approach to Heart • Selected Essays (ebook) | Brasstown Press |

# ACKNOWLEDGMENTS

Thanks to Karen Stafford for providing the Foreword, while exemplifying grace under pressure.

Thanks to Isabel McNeill Carley's friends and former colleagues for their encouragement and feedback. Thanks, in particular, to Judith Thomas Solomon for kind permission to reproduce her unforgettable portrait of Betsy Higginbottam.

Thanks to the American Orff-Schulwerk Association, the American Recorder Society, and the Association of Disciple Musicians for their permissions to re-purpose previously published materials.

Edited and produced by Brasstown Press with production assistance from Hannah Bornhofen, Robin Yeh, and Sloan Christopher.

## Note on this edition

This book retains all the positive traits of the underlying materials. Inconsistencies and introduced errors are the sole responsibility of the editors. Special thanks to John Stryder.

$\sim AMC$

www.ingramcontent.com/pod-product-compliance
Lightning Source LLC
Chambersburg PA
CBHW032052090426
42744CB00005B/186